Black Men Changing the Narrative Through Education

by Walter R. McCollum, PhD
Foreword by Elder André Lynch

Published by

McCollum Enterprises, LLC

Walter R. McCollum, PhD

Fort Washington, Maryland

ISBN 978-0-9791406-9-3

All Rights Reserved, Copyright 2018

No part of this book may be reproduced or transmitted in any form or by any means, graphic, electronic, or mechanical, including photocopying, recording, taping, or by any information storage retrieval system, without permission in writing from the publisher.

Dedication

But those who hope in the LORD will renew their strength. They will soar on wings like eagles; they will run and not grow weary, they will walk and not be faint.
—Isaiah 40:31

Thank you, God, for providing me with renewed strength to continue the journey of life. Because I look to the hills from which cometh my help, I am able to conquer the world! Because of your anointing and favor, I am able to be a beacon of light to others who need inspiration and hope! Because of your love, I am able to give selflessly to others from a pure place! Thank you for providing me with the opportunity to be a demonstration of service. I will forever serve, praise, and honor you.

This book is dedicated to all who have been on the move to uplift African American males through education, community, and service. Also, to those who are inspired by role models, mentors, and EXCEPTIONAL human beings

. . . educated African American males who are using their lives to impact positive social change.

Be joyful in hope, patient in affliction, faithful in prayer.
—Romans 12:12

Acknowledgments

To all of the pastors and spiritual advisors who have demonstrated what it looks like to be an educated African American male on a mission to be used as a vessel to change some aspect of the world. Your model of service has helped shape my passion to influence positive social change! I am indebted to you forever.

To the contributors of this book, thank you for your support and for all that you do to use your journey as a life-altering tactic to effect positive change in the world.

Special thanks to my editor, Toni Williams. Thank you so much for supporting this book project. You are phenomenal! I am very thankful for you.

Table of Contents

Foreword ix

Introduction 1

1 Changing the Narrative of Black Male College Achievement 7

2 Dr. William L. Quisenberry 17

3 Dr. Pettis D. Perry 61

4 Victor Arthur, PhD 91

5 Dr. Calvin Nobles 109

6 Chernoh Wurie, PhD 125

7 Dr. Brian Grizzell 141

8 Dr. Ben Magee 156

9 John C. Lofton, III, PhD 173

10 Quentin Newhouse, Jr., PhD, PCC, CPC 183

11 Dr. Terrance Knox 194

12 Otis Johnson, PhD, MPA 207

13 Jonas Nguh, PhD, RN 223

14 Walter R. McCollum, PhD 239

About the Author 253

Foreword

From an educational perspective, two things must be considered relative to information – acquisition and appropriation. Achievement is the careful blend of these two ideas that yields success as an outcome. Higher education involves the acquisition of information. The greater call to answer involves a careful, yet successful, appropriation of information that changes lives for the better. Higher education becomes a platform whereby the Black man can emerge as a vessel of power through wisdom. According to Luke 12:48, to whom much is given, much is required. Through their testimonials, Black men of higher education leave a legacy whereby others can navigate toward power and success.

Through this book, Dr. McCollum reaches back and deposits the pearls of wisdom he has gained from higher education into the lives of other academics. As a man of reputation, respect, and resilience, he allows other Black men to shine the light into their own lives and share their educational experiences with the world. Get ready to soar and reach your greatest potential as you immerse yourself into the invaluable content of this book!

—Elder André R. Lynch

Introduction

Men of color are changing their own narratives through education. Black men are using higher education as a gateway to affect positive social change.
—Dr. Walter McCollum

The focus of this book is to show a different view of Black males on their quest to become game changers through higher education. For decades, Black males' absence from college enrollment, underachievement, and low rates of baccalaureate degree completion have been among the most pressing and complex issues in higher education. More troubling than the problems themselves is the way they have been mishandled by educators and policy makers. Capitalizing on the troubled status of Black male students in higher education has yielded few solutions. Thus, educational outcomes for this population have remained stagnant due to the deficit orientation that is constantly reinforced in media, academic journals, and educational practice.

There is a lot to learn from Black men who have been successful. To increase their educational attainment, the common one-sided emphasis on failure and low-performing Black male undergraduates must be counterbalanced with insights and demonstrations from those who somehow managed to navigate their way to and through higher education, despite all that is stacked against them – low teacher expectations, insufficient academic preparation for college-level work, racist and culturally unresponsive college environments, and the debilitating consequences of underrepresentation, to name a few.

This book consists of personal testaments from selected Black men who not only earned a higher education, but also used their education to effect positive social change. In the National Black Male College Achievement Study conducted in 2012, 219 students who were successful in higher and postsecondary settings were interviewed and had a lot to share about the personal, familial, and institutional enablers of their achievement. Truth be told, that side of the story is quite impressive, more so than the problems and inequities that are typically amplified in research journals, policy reports, and the media. These problems and inequities include the following:

- Only 47% of Black male students graduated on time from U.S. high schools in 2008, compared to 78% of White males (Schott Foundation for Public Education, 2010).
- Black male students are often comparatively less prepared than are others for the rigors of college level academic work (Bonner & Bailey, 2006; Loury, 2004; Lundy-Wagner & Gasman, 2011; Palmer, Davis, & Hilton, 2009).
- In 2002, Black men comprised only 4.3% of students enrolled at institutions of higher education, which is exactly the same percentage as in 1976 (Harper, 2006a; Strayhorn, 2010).
- Black men are overrepresented on revenue-generating intercollegiate sports teams. In 2009, they comprised only 3.6% of undergraduate students, but 55.3% of football and basketball players at public NCAA Division I institutions (Harper, 2012).
- Black male college completion rates are lowest among both sexes and all racial/ethnic groups in U.S. higher education (Harper, 2006a; Strayhorn, 2010).

- Across four cohorts of undergraduates, the 6-year graduation rate for Black male students attending public colleges and universities was 33.3%, compared to 48.1% for students overall (Harper, 2012).
- Black men's degree attainment across all levels of postsecondary education is alarmingly low, especially in comparison to their same-race female counterparts (U.S. Department of Education, 2010).
- Black men's representation in graduate and professional school lags behind that of their Latino and Asian American male counterparts. For example, between 1977 and 2007, Black men experienced a 109% increase in post-baccalaureate degree attainment, compared to 242% for Latino men and 425% for Asian American men; the comparative rate of increase for Black women was 253% (Harper & Davis, 2012).
- Black undergraduate men, like other racial minority students at predominately White institutions, routinely encounter racist stereotypes and racial microagressions that undermine their achievement and sense of belonging (Bonner, 2010; Harper,

2009; Singer, 2005; Smith, Allen, & Danley, 2007; Smith, Yosso, & Solorzano, 2007).
- In comparison to their same-race female counterparts, Black men take fewer notes in class, spend less time writing papers and competing class assignments, participate less frequently in college activities, hold fewer leadership positions, and report lower grades (Cuyjet, 1997; Harper Carina, Bridges, & Hayek, 2004).

These problems warrant ongoing scholarly examination, intervention, and strategic institutional leadership, as well as greater transparency, accountability, and policy responses. However, instructive insights from Black men who have experienced college differently – those who actually enrolled, were actively engaged inside and outside the classroom, did well academically, graduated, and went on to pursue additional degrees beyond the baccalaureate – are also warranted. Unfortunately, their journeys to and through college have been overshadowed by the aforementioned statistics. This book shares a different story – many different stories – and celebrates African American male doctors who are changing the narrative by achieving a higher education to change the world!

References

Harper, S. R. (2012). *Black male student success in higher education: A report from the National Black Male College Achievement Study.* Philadelphia: University of Pennsylvania, Center for the Study of Race and Equity in Education.

1
Changing the Narrative of Black Male College Achievement

Education is the most powerful weapon, which you can use to change the world
　　　　　　　　　　—Honorable Nelson Mandela

More and more Black men are earning higher education. The National Black Male College Achievement Study highlighted the narratives of 219 Black male achievers selected from six types of institutions (small liberal arts colleges, large public research universities, private research universities, state universities, and private and public Historically Black Colleges and Universities [HBCUs]) to participate in the study. From the interviews conducted, a key finding that related to going to college was that, from boyhood through high school, parents and other family members reinforced to the achievers that college was the most viable pathway to social uplift and success. Although they had little or no firsthand experience with higher education, these parents cultivated within their children a belief that college was the only allowable next step after high school. Most of the achievers' parents and family members aggressively sought out educational resources to ensure the achievers' success through tutoring and academic support programs, college preparatory initiatives, and summer academies and camps.

Educators, administrators, and others are continually working to improve Black male student success and degree attainment rates. At the individual level, student organizations are common at many universities and can be an affirming, supportive way to help Black men navigate the process of earning a degree and to provide them with a ready-made peer group. For example, Harvard's Black Men forum is a university organization founded and led by students. Its purpose is to provide a venue for conversations on topics of cultural significance, including race, gender, and academic experiences at Harvard, as well as world politics. Several other institutions have collegiate chapters of the 100 Black Men of America. Students in groups such as these often advise each other on navigating the university, responding productively to racism and racial stereotypes, and using important institutional resources

Some institutions have convened internal and external stakeholders to consider the theme of Black male success. For example, the University of Akron hosts the annual Black Male Summit to bring educators, administrators, students, and community members from across Ohio and neighboring states. The summit includes high-profile keynote speakers and workshops with a customized track for students and another track for professionals and citizens concerned about student success.

Many universities have also convened stakeholders as part of broader initiatives that include longer term activities. One example is the University of California, Los Angeles (UCLA) Black Male Institute (BMI), which is directed by a tenured professor who brings together more than 20 undergraduates and graduate students to conduct practical, useful research and interventions that aim to improve the educational and social status of Black male students across all levels of education. BMI engages educational leaders, community members, and policy makers, as well as expert scholars at and beyond UCLA. More than 500 middle and high school students have gone to UCLA to participate in BMI workshops on preparing for college, and hundreds of educators and community members have attended BMI's annual Black Male Think Tank Conference. These types of initiatives can go beyond current undergraduate enrollment to prepare Black men for graduate school and beyond.

Another way of formalizing a focus on Black men is to create credit-bearing courses with culturally sensitive curricula targeted toward helping Black men adjust to college life and learning. For example, Wake Forest University, the University of Southern California, UCLA, and the University of Pennsylvania offer courses designed to facilitate learning, critical reflection, and dialogue about the status and experiences of Black undergraduate men. A key activity of these courses is acquainting Black male students with institutional resources that help ensure successful transitions, engagement, academic success, and persistence toward degree attainment. Some institutions have integrated their efforts within a formal structure. For example, the Todd. A. Bell National Resource Center on the African American Male at the Ohio State University and the Center for Male Engagement at the Community College of Philadelphia consist of full-time professors with efforts ranging from outreach to Black male high school students to analyze and report on institutional data on trends in Black male student outcomes.

Beyond institutional efforts, federal and state policy makers, higher education associations, the NCAA, foundations, and others have several ways to respond to social, political, and economic threats to Black male student success and college completion. This is not to suggest that these efforts should replace the initiatives currently offered on college and university campuses, but both institutional and policy responses are necessary to improve Black men's educational outcomes and post-secondary-degree attainment rates. Drawing from existing research and promising practices from institutional initiatives, the following recommendations are examples of ways to complement institutional efforts with new policies, practices, and resources, thereby changing the narrative of Black men's success in higher education:

- **Increase Investments in College Preparation Programs** – Given the key role of these programs in supporting academically prepared students from underserved populations, federal and state policy makers, institutional leaders, and community-based organizations can play a key role by supporting and advocating on behalf of college outreach and preparation initiatives, particularly during times of fiscal exigency, when these resources are especially vulnerable to budget cuts or elimination.

- **Address Funding Inequities That Disadvantage Public HBCUs** – A 2006 study of 19 southern states revealed "public 4-year HBCUs are the only sector of higher education in which Blacks consistently approach or achieve equity in enrollment and degree completion. Moreover, HBCUs outperform predominantly White institutions proportionately in graduating and preparing Black students for careers in high-need industries, such as the health professions and the science, technology, engineering and math fields, despite enrolling a significantly higher proportion of first-generation students and Pell Grant recipients.

- **Increase Federal and State Financial Aid for Lower-Income Black Male Students** – Many students who drop out of college do so because they cannot afford the cost. Financial aid plays a significant role in Black men's persistence and academic success, especially at highly selective institutions.

- **Match Incarceration and Educational Investments** – The U.S. Department of Justice estimates that 85,600 Black Men between the ages of 18 and 24 (the traditional college-age population) were serving sentences in federal and state prisons in 2010. On average, taxpayers paid $32,226 that year per inmate. State policy makers should enact an investment strategy that matches taxpayer dollars spent on incarcerating 18- to 24-year-old Black men with race- and gender-specific efforts that improve their pathways to and through college.

- **Require Assessment in State-Funded Initiatives** – Institutions receiving state funds for any Black male initiative must use a core set of standards for alignment and assessment. Consistent standards should be used as a framework for program design, reporting, evaluation, and other efforts to document effectiveness and ensure accountability.

- **Establish Consortia in Public Secondary Systems** – It is imperative to establish and support consortia such as the Arkansas African-American Male Initiative and system-wide efforts such as the City University of New York's Black Male Initiative and the University System of Georgia's African-American Male Initiative. Such collaborative efforts can facilitate information and resource sharing among institutions and better equip them to address systemic barriers to Black men's postsecondary success.

- **Develop a National Study that Monitors College Access and Success of Minority Males** – The Higher Education Opportunity Act of 2008 requires the U.S. Department of Education to conduct a study on the state of academic achievement for underrepresented males, with a particular focus on Black and Hispanic students. This mandated study represents an opportunity to conduct further research on minority male college access and success and to make recommendations to Congress and state superintendents of education on new approaches to increase the number of Black and Hispanic males preparing for college, graduating, and successfully entering careers where they are most underrepresented.

- **Require Transparency in College Athletics** – State policy makers and system-level leaders should require public institutions to collect, analyze, and publish data annually concerning the overrepresentation of Black men among revenue-generating college student athletes, as well as the racial and gender disparities in graduation rates. Institutions that show inequities from year to year should be required to submit a plan for reversing these problematic trends.

- **Promote Policies and Practices that Advance Equity** – Over the past decade, affirmative action policies and race-conscious practices in university admissions have been intensely scrutinized and eliminated in some states. A substantial body of empirical research confirms that institutional diversity and inclusion is beneficial to the learning, growth, and development of all college students. Thus, policy makers at all levels must be willing to defend race- and gender-conscious initiatives on college and university campuses.

- **Reclaim Near-Completers** – In September 2011, policy makers and other stakeholders attended the National Summit on Near Completion. The meeting focused on students who have left colleges and universities without earning their degrees, but are eligible to receive associate's degrees or, with assistance, can complete the few remaining courses required to earn bachelor's degrees. Federal and state policy makers should aim to reclaim Black men who discontinued college enrollment and help them construct plans to complete their degrees.

The aforementioned recommendations are far from exhaustive. No single initiative is likely to be sufficient at any university with racial and gender inequities that disfavor Black male students. The array of policy-relevant challenges that undermine young Black men's educational attainment and social mobility requires a substantive policy agenda that includes, but extends far beyond, the aforementioned recommendations to support changing the narrative of Black male success in higher education.

In the upcoming chapters, you will hear the amazing stories of Black Male doctoral degree holders. These men have not only earned a doctoral degree, but are using their educational experience to change the world. Their journeys have not been easy, but they are changing the narrative of Black male college achievement for generations to come.

2
Dr. William L. Quisenberry

Educator/Consultant
Servant Consultant Group

Everybody can be great . . . because anybody can serve. You do not have to have a college degree to serve. You do not have to make your subject and verb agree to serve. You only need a heart full of grace. A soul generated by love.
—Dr. Martin Luther King, Jr.

Introduction

My name is William L. Quisenberry, and I am from Lexington, Kentucky. My background includes studying and practicing within the field of business administration, coordinating implementation projects for Fortune 500 clients, overseeing vendors and suppliers, project management, research and analysis, consulting, and corporate training. I have collaborated and worked with a variety of major organizations that include Accenture, Army Core of Engineers, Best Buy, Branch Banking and Trust, Halliburton, IBM, John Hancock Financial, Lexmark International, Lockheed Martin, U.S. Department of Veterans Affairs, Wal-Mart, and World Trade Center Association. I have also worked with more than 12 universities teaching, mentoring, and supervising dissertation and thesis research or serving as a subject matter expert or consultant.

I hold a bachelor's of business administration (BBA) degree in finance, a BBA in marketing, and a master's of business administration from Sullivan University's Graduate School of Business. I completed my doctor of business administration (DBA) degree with a specialization in leadership at Walden University's College of Management & Technology. My dissertation was titled, *Common Characteristics and Attributes of Self-Managed Virtual Teams*. I have received over 50 double-blind peer-reviewed full paper acceptances that have been presented or published or are in the process of being published in research journals, conference proceedings, periodicals, or book projects. I have chaired, co-chaired, and served as a member or reviewer on over 150 dissertation research committees.

I have been very fortunate and blessed in life. If someone would have told me I would go on to accomplish some of these goals and milestones when I was younger, I would have called that person a liar. However, despite all these accomplishments, there is still a lot of work to be done. There is a critical need in our nation for mentorship, guidance, justice, mercy, and faith. Education has played an instrumental role in my life and continues to be a major part of my existence, as I work in various academic settings. I am a strong advocate for others pursuing higher education, as it truly offers the opportunity to reach a level of success that may not be available otherwise.

In this chapter, I seek to uncover and present the responsibilities associated with obtaining higher learning. I propose that higher education is not for the recipient alone, but for others as well. If we are going to transform African American communities and the world at large, we African Americans must embrace giving back, coming back, and engaging within the Black community. In this chapter, I share some of my own influences, challenges, and experiences associated with the journey of achieving academic and professional success, while also presenting an overarching challenge and call to action for everyone within the African American community, especially African American men. We have an unfulfilled mission in front of us. Will you accept the call?

Influences From Parents and Grandparents

My greatest childhood influence that sparked my connection to higher education was my parents. My father required his children to put forth maximum time, effort, and energy regarding our schoolwork, studies, and education. Although we did not always fully adhere to the demands from our mother and father to focus on our studies, there still was a connection and level of importance planted within us because of the time, attention, and energy my parents placed upon educational activities.

Other familial influences included my patriarchal grandparents. My grandparents grew up in racially segregated and openly oppressive times in Kentucky, but still found a way to strive, persevere, and accomplish remarkable milestones. My grandfather, William Thomas Quisenberry, Sr., was drafted into the Army to serve in World War II before he even finished high school. Despite being deployed and not finishing high school, he finished his studies after he returned and earned a trade certificate from the Lincoln Institute, an African American educational training center.

My grandmother, Gloria Patten Quisenberry, attended college, which was very unusual for Black women of her time. She attended Kentucky State University (K-State) in Frankfort, which was, and is, a historically Black college and university (HBCU). She received her degree in business administration in the 1940s while studying at K-State. She often told stories of how strict HBCUs were during this period, how serious it was for African Americans to be attending school and the dignity and respect that was associated with the opportunity.

University was not a place for partying or socializing, although I assume it did happen to some extent. Having the opportunity to attend college meant that you had been selected, along with a handful of other fortunate individuals, to receive specialized training. However, with the honor came an immense amount of pressure and responsibility to help your people progress and to offer opportunities to those coming behind you. The mentality was not to receive training and an education, get a good-paying job, move to the suburbs, and forget about the friends, family, and oppressed individuals you left behind. Rather, a major objective of receiving a higher education was to be empowered to be a change agent, to help provide a pathway for others, and to serve as a key that would help to combat injustice and unlock new opportunities and freedoms for others in oppressed minority groups, specifically African Americans.

My grandmother told stories in which she compared attending an HBCU during this period to boarding or even military school. There were not only educators and professors, but mentors, tutors, and supervisors on campus. Students were taught not only academic and professional disciplines, but also the proper etiquette to follow when attending dinners, balls, or special events, as well as spiritual guidance and much more. The goal of HBCUs was to make students into well-rounded, educated, disciplined change agents who could penetrate mainstream culture and territory and bring about positive change.

My grandparents accomplished their goals and fulfilled their assignments. They were leaders, mentors, and pinnacles in their community for many years. My grandmother became a budget analyst with the Bluegrass Army Depot outside of Lexington, Kentucky. She had a long and successful career in a leadership position with the federal government. She was amazing at her work, was respected by peers and colleagues of all colors, and retired with great honor. My grandfather retired from the same Army Depot as a warehouse forklift driver. Both of my grandparents worked very hard to help other African Americans get good-paying jobs with various organizations. They were well-respected mentors and guides for many within the community. They were blessed to receive an education, but they saw it as a responsibility to help others, and they fulfilled their mission. This backdrop, these stories, and the examples I saw of their leadership, along with my parents, influenced me significantly. They showed me the importance and emphasis of education, without needing to verbally express it.

Childhood Influences From the Late 80s and Early 90s

Another family influence was my older brother, Randall Quisenberry, Jr. There was quite an age gap between my oldest brother and me. He was preparing to graduate high school when I was about 6 years old. My brother graduated high school during the "A Different World" era. "A Different World" was a television show that chronicled the lives of young African Americans from various walks of life (urban, rural, rich, poor, middle class) who all met at a fictional HBCU named Hillman College. The show was a spinoff of "The Cosby Show," and aired from 1987 to 1993. The premise of the show originally centered on Denise Huxtable (from "The Cosby Show") going to college at Hillman and chronicled her experience along with the experiences of other characters from different walks of life. The show's popularity continued even after the actress playing Denise left the show.

The show discussed issues, challenges, and experiences that had not been addressed by "The Cosby Show" or any other network television programs during this era. It showed the challenges of being a young, African American, while also showing the joys and triumphs involved with pursuing higher education, specifically at HBCUs. Bill

Cosby, the creator of "A Different World," was a strong proponent and supporter of HBCUs, and often wore paraphernalia for different Black colleges and universities on "The Cosby Show" as free advertisement and support. "A Different World" took this support to a new level. Because of the success of the television show, enrollment rates among young African Americans at colleges, and specifically at HBCUs, skyrocketed during the late 80s and early 90s. It is unclear how many lives were inspired by, and forever changed, because of "A Different World," although I can certainly say that, as a young child, I was thrilled by the thought of attending college because of this show, even though I did not fully understand what college was at the time. A seed was planted by this television series at a very young age.

My oldest brother Randall was also influenced by "A Different World" and was inspired to attend college. He attended my grandmother's alma mater, K-State from 1988 to 1992 and graduated with a bachelor's degree in math. He was in a joint program that allowed him to obtain a bachelor's degree in math and transfer to an affiliated university to obtain a master's degree in engineering. Still having an absolute joy and love for the Black college experience, he attended Florida A&M University in Tallahassee, Florida, for his graduate studies. He ultimately changed course after attending Florida A&M from 1992 to 1994 and no longer desired to pursue engineering. Instead, he felt a calling to do ministry and teach. He started serving as a minister at a church in Tallahassee, received his teaching certificate, and has been teaching middle and high school math for almost 20 years.

He also returned to K-State and completed a master's degree in education. A major focus of his teaching and ministry is working with underserved, at-risk, inner-city youth. He currently teaches at-risk youth at an alternative high school in Jacksonville, Florida, and is heavily engaged in outreach and inner-city ministry within Jacksonville. He was a strong influence on my decision to pursue higher education, teach, and reach back to underserved communities.

My brother is also currently working toward a doctor of education degree. He has completed his coursework and comprehensive exams and is about a year into his dissertation coursework. He is scheduled to finish his dissertation within the next year. Although I am younger and I was inspired by my older brother to pursue higher education, I was blessed to receive my doctoral degree first, which in turn influenced him to pursue his doctorate as well. I have had the opportunity to offer feedback and coaching to my brother on the dissertation process, as it is something that I have also been through and have successfully mentored many others as well. Thus, we have been able to contribute to one another's success.

Community and Mentoring Influences

Community leaders and professionals visited my schools when I was growing up. I also heard speeches in class and had experiences with mentors. The fact that there were not many visits from African American men who shared their experiences as educated professionals within the community was discouraging. I do remember attending an inner-city middle school in a low-income neighborhood that had a lot of crime, poverty, and social challenges, and we had a temporary tutor or mentor.

I do not recall his name, but he was an undergraduate student at the University of Kentucky, which was a research institution in Lexington, where I grew up. The young man was studying social work and was from

Chicago. He shared his experiences of growing up in a violent, inner-city neighborhood within Chicago and highlighted how he was able to make it out of the negative environment he experienced growing up.

He had instant credibility with my fellow classmates and me. He was intelligent, yet still cool; furthermore, he had experienced a similar environment to the one we were living in, although it was likely far worse. He understood our lingo, culture, feelings, and experiences, but he was also a student at our state's flagship research institution. He not only understood our culture, "the streets," and current events, but he was in college, which was something that I thought was a distant dream at that point in my life.

While I do not remember this young man's name, I do recall that he had a profound impact on me. There was something about working with him over the course of that semester; being able to connect with him and learn from his tutoring and mentorship; and watching how he interacted and engaged with others that had a lasting impact on me.

A similar experience involved my high school social worker, Mr. Steve Duerson, who was also an African American male. Mr. Duerson took the time to mentor me through my high school studies, and he was responsible for taking me on my first college visit to the University of Kentucky. Because he was a graduate of the university, he was able to introduce me to the leadership team within Minority Affairs, Admissions, and other departments within the university. He also helped me gather all the forms I would need to apply to the university and even offered assistance with the documentation and steps involved in the process. He played an instrumental role in helping me be accepted to the University of Kentucky when I graduated from high school.

One of the lasting impressions that Mr. Duerson left on my life was the responsibility of giving back to others and service. While he was mentoring me, he also made sure that I mentored others. I was a part of a special program where a select group of African American males from our high school would go to elementary and middle schools and mentor other African American kids. Thus, although we were only high school students ourselves, we were taught to mentor those coming behind us. I will never forget my time in this program, working with young Black kids who were growing up in very tough conditions, single-parent homes, low-income environments, etc. Seeing the joy these kids would show when we would walk into the classroom to pull them out for our one-on-one mentoring and tutoring time left a lasting impact and helped me understand the value that time and mentorship truly offer. The facilitators of these programs tracked the data very closely, and the results included increased attendance, reports from parents regarding their kids' behavior at home, and increased academic performance because of the mentoring program. Spending only a few hours per week provided all of these results. It certainly resonated with me and left an impression.

My relationship with Mr. Duerson continued after I moved on to the University of Kentucky as an undergraduate. He would have me come back to the high school frequently to engage in mentoring programs, speak to classes and groups of other African Americans, and continue giving back. I was also responsible for helping juniors and seniors to navigate the college application, admission, and assimilation process. Most of my mentoring time was spent with African American males, since the organizers were putting a lot of emphasis on recruiting more Black males into higher education.

I also had other influences in my life similar to Mr. Duerson, including my high school counselor Mrs. Clay, my African American history teacher Mrs. Akins, and far too many others to name here. What was clear from individuals like my parents, grandparents, older siblings, art and media like "A Different World" and "The Cosby Show," the young mentor that I had while in middle school, and my African American social workers, counselors, and teachers who pushed me to my full potential while ensuring that I understood the responsibility that came along with success was that most of these influences and experiences centered around education. I often had these life-changing experiences as I was pursuing education or as I was being encouraged to continue pursuing more learning opportunities while giving back. Education was a common theme woven throughout these experiences, and because of that, I quickly and clearly understood its importance. As a result, a lasting connection was sparked and continues to ignite a deep fire within.

Challenges and Stories of Perseverance While Pursuing Higher Education

Pursuing education, especially higher education, has not been easy. I had some learning challenges as a kid that would often rear their ugly head during my educational journey. Whether it was a slight dyslexic disorder, a short attention span, severe eye challenges and diseases, or the resulting migraine headaches, there were plenty of opportunities to create excuses. After combining these issues with the resulting insecurities that contributed to a disdain for public speaking and an extremely introverted personality, it was easy to conclude that I was not likely heading for academic success.

However, along with the challenges came a strong curiosity, desire to learn, joy of reading (or at least listening to great speakers and thought leaders if the eye challenges had become too much), and ultimately a joy of writing and what appeared to be a gift to write. I did not recognize the gift of writing I possessed. Rather, my teachers, mentors, professors, and so forth saw the potential much sooner than I did. I would often receive compelling remarks on paper reviews and was encouraged to continue writing more by teachers and colleagues.

The joy I experienced while learning, my curiosity, and my writing ability have ultimately been some of my natural secret weapons. I have always been able to put in more hours (which were often required) to learn the material or complete projects. I sometimes felt as though I was not the best verbal communicator, lecturer, or speech giver, but I was capable of very solid writing, so I sought to make the best out of the opportunities I had to write, instead of putting emphasis on public speaking.

I also leveraged my desire, comfort, and ability to listen to others to my advantage. Listening is a lost art, and is becoming less prevalent and less used on a daily basis due to society's obsession with everyone having a voice. Much of this has occurred because of social media, where anyone can write a quick thought, hop on a live video feed, or record a message and post it for others to see. Although there are certainly benefits from so many people having a voice, we may be neglecting our ability to *listen* to all these voices. There are many voices or individuals who are saying a lot, but really have very little of value to add to the discussion. Too many voices equates to too much noise, and a growing number of individuals want to speak but do not want to listen.

I tend to be a little different in this regard, as I enjoy having the opportunity to listen, instead of speak. I leveraged this gift of listening throughout my studies (although I can easily drift off due to my sometimes short attention span, so focused and engaged listening does take real effort), and I believe it has already paid off and continues to offer major dividends.

To summarize the strategic approach that I used in my academic pursuits and continue to leverage in my life, I would say leverage your strengths and seek to mitigate the implications of your weaknesses. This is not anything new. Organizations, individuals, and athletic teams all seek to use this strategic approach to capitalize on opportunities while mitigating weaknesses and threats. However, despite the simplicity in theory, the application and continued use of this model is still undervalued and not leveraged as often as it should be. If you can consistently evaluate your strengths and weaknesses in a relevant context, which means applying the concept to where you are in life while truly *acting* upon the details, you will greatly increase your chances of being successful, whether in higher education, community development, work, or family affairs. Of course everything will not be perfect, but it will increase your ability to capitalize upon opportunities while mitigating risks, which equates to increasing your chances of reaching goals and targets. This was the model I used to overcome my own challenges while pursuing higher education.

Educational Influence on My Professional Career

My educational career greatly influenced my professional career, and they are ultimately one and the same. I am currently an educator, mentor, coach, researcher, and consultant. Whether I am serving as a faculty member, a professional coach, a dissertation mentor; engaging on a research initiative; acting as a small business consultant; or being involved in grassroots community development and outreach efforts, my educational career is instrumental in them all.

My educational career provides a strong foundation in research, critical thinking, intense reading and writing if required, and much more. The experiences of working with diverse groups of people from varying backgrounds, faiths, demographics, countries, disciplines, and professions help me embrace and enjoy diversity and inclusion. My educational career provides me with a level of comfort engaging with others on intense issues or topics, taking complex concepts and breaking them down for others to understand, and building others up to pursue more in life.

My educational career has helped to inspire and shape me into a social change agent, and this is exactly what I consider myself to be engaged in professionally in some form. Whether helping a homeless person get a meal, sharing my faith in Jesus Christ via the Gospel, engaging in outreach initiatives within subsidized housing projects, sitting on a board for a social services organization, teaching management and leadership in higher education, or working with small business owners to improve their strategic planning, all of these actions and activities center on positive social and human change. Pursuing higher education and any learning experience will bring about a level of change within a person. Therefore, as an educator, I help others experience a level of change in varying facets on a daily basis. I am so blessed to be alive and living this amazing dream!

Characteristics and Attributes That Contributed to My Educational Success

Wise – Having a lot of information without the ability to process, organize, and act upon it can be pointless. This is what makes an information technology system such as Google so useful. It takes mass amounts of information and data, categorizes and optimizes it based upon keyword searches, and gives the information to users when they request it. Wisdom is similar. Wisdom is the ability to take information and transform it into useful knowledge. It involves taking data and changing the data into useful material that is understood and recollected and, potentially most important, can be acted upon. Having the ability to be wise in certain situations, circumstances, and environments, even when they were outside of my norm, has been a huge benefit in my life. I am not foolish enough to believe that I am the wisest person or a guru, but I've been blessed with wisdom when I needed it most, and it has certainly allowed me to excel or at least to survive in various environments. My favorite thing about wisdom is that if you need more of it, you can just simply ask: "If any of you lacks wisdom, let him ask God, who gives generously to all without reproach, and it will be given him" (James 1:5, ESV).

Disciplined – It is difficult to achieve any milestones or goals or to have sustainable success without some form of discipline. The same goes with academic and professional careers, and discipline has played a major role in my life. When pursuing higher education, it is important to find a level of consistency and do some activities that you do not enjoy or do not feel like doing or maybe engage in some activities that you are not very good at. You must possess the strength to continue striving, pushing, and remaining consistent while pursuing your goals. I was blessed to have a father who served in the U.S. Army within the 101st Airborne division, did two tours in Vietnam, and was a drill sergeant for many years. Discipline was embedded in our household growing up, and this paid massive dividends in my life. Additionally, I was heavily engaged in several sports activities growing up, especially football. Discipline is a major aspect of football, and through football, I had an opportunity to get used to doing things that I did not necessarily enjoy, but knew they had to be done in a particular manner and within a certain timeline. This character trait and attribute followed me into my higher education pursuits and helped me ensure I met deadlines and followed grading rubrics and guidelines.

Scholarly – It is difficult, and maybe impossible, to achieve certain academic accomplishments, especially at the graduate level, without embracing scholarship. Higher education is not something that can be completely winged without cracking the books. You will have to engage in some sort of serious academic study if you are going to successfully complete the journey and if you plan to get something out of your degree program besides a piece of paper. Some students focus only on getting the piece of paper, but I see that as a waste of time, energy, and opportunities to learn and grow. I certainly had friends, especially while we were undergrads, who seemed gifted enough to wing their way through school. They would party, goof off, and relax and still seemed to be able to cram just in time for the exam and pass. This was not my testimony. I was not as gifted. If I was going to pass an exam, I really had to work hard. As you go deeper into your academic pursuits to graduate school, or even within many undergraduate programs, it is becoming less and less about passing exams and more about applying what you are learning via projects, presentations, and in-depth and scholarly research papers. As a result, it is almost impossible to complete an academic degree program without embracing scholarship. Being scholarly has been a blessing for me, not only academically, but also in life. We live in a day and age where things are changing rapidly. Therefore, you need to embrace scholarship and study to stay ahead of the curve.

Systematic – When seeking to start a journey, a blueprint, roadmap, plan, and system can all be helpful. Being methodological and following a system can help you streamline your actions; reduce ambiguity; and add clarity, strength, guidance, and momentum, even while pursuing higher education. I felt like a fish out of water when I first attended college, despite having known others who had taken the journey prior to me. I knew that I was not the first to undertake this journey, and therefore I did not need to recreate the wheel. I relied heavily upon university staff, mentors, upperclassmen, guides, and policy handbooks to help me navigate each degree program, position, or project I found myself engaged in. Being systematic can improve your chances of completing your academic journey and achieving your goals. However, do not limit yourself to systems. There are times when systems are outdated, do not make sense, are broken, or have been designed to hinder you or hold you back rather than propel you forward. It is at this point that some of the other traits that I have discussed can be useful, such as being wise, disciplined, scholarly, and even patient. You have to know when to avoid, reengineer, and circumvent a system that is no longer relevant to your particular circumstance or is becoming a hindrance. Despite the challenges that can arise from embracing a systematic approach, the advantages often far outweigh the disadvantages and can save you a lot of time and many headaches. I have seen many positive results stem from systematic behaviors and attributes.

Patient – No matter how systematic you are, life does not always go according to plan. There will be challenges, setbacks, delays, unjust persecution, misunderstandings, and more. You will miss the mark, make mistakes, and sometimes really blow it. I have experienced all of these challenges and then some. When challenges do arise, you have to find a way to keep your cool, remain calm, and get back on track as soon as possible. I like to summarize many of these behaviors as being patient. Anytime you are pursuing major milestones, goals, or accomplishments or when you have big dreams – which I think everyone should have – you will also need to have a certain level of patience or you will become a mad, hysterical, resentful, cynical, condescending jerk that nobody wants to be around or collaborate with. You will lose the energy, drive, and meaning behind your original goals and dreams and will be much more likely to give up. Being patient does not mean that you do not experience setbacks or disappointments, or even that you will not temporarily turn into the jerk mentioned above. Despite the challenges, mistakes, and frustrations experienced, patient people find a way to bounce back and get on track. Patience is a virtue that will bring forth a lot of fruit and synergy in your life. I recommend pursuing patience, which is not always fun to do and often occurs after persevering through challenges, pain, and heartache, but also surrounding yourself with patient individuals. Patience and humility tend to coexist, because the process of achieving both is similar. The process may not be fun, but it is useful in the end. Additionally, patience adds synergy to other character traits and attributes. It acts as a kind of glue to hold them together with the others.

How Higher Education Contributed to My Personal and Professional Growth

Earning a higher education has allowed me to become more comfortable with being uncomfortable. This is constantly a work in progress, but the experience of pursuing multiple higher education degrees, especially a doctorate, brings a certain level of fortitude, confidence, and ability to embrace the unknown. I am sure that my faith system and beliefs also have a major influence in this regard.

Many never seek to pursue new opportunities, to learn, or to go against the status quo or norms of society out of fear of the unknown and discomfort. Always wanting to fit in with the crowd, the latest trends, societal norms, and so forth is enough to derail even the most experienced people. This is where issues such as herd thinking come into fruition. Adults sometimes give the impression, either by mistake or on purpose, that these types of peer pressure are only prevalent among youth and maybe very young adults, but this is purely a myth.

Higher education has allowed me to have many different experiences, meet many different types of individuals, and push my own capabilities, attributes, and skills to the limit. Many of these experiences were uncomfortable for me and far outside my own comfort zone. As a result, I was forced to grow and learn how to be comfortable in uncomfortable situations, environments, and circumstances; to rely upon my faith in God; embrace ongoing and continuous learning and improvement; and find a suitable outcome or resolution to the challenges before me.

I have also learned how to avoid always seeking to resolve what appears to be a challenge or problem and instead to potentially change my outlook of, or viewpoint on, the situation. These types of behaviors, practices, and skills can be learned, developed, and improved upon. Pursuing higher learning has helped to shape these abilities and practices, while bringing weaknesses and opportunities for improvement to the surface. This has continued to have a lasting impact on me and on my work as an individual.

Post-Degree Obstacles

One of the greatest challenges I have had to overcome after earning a college degree, specifically my doctorate, was redefining success. When I first obtained my doctorate, I thought the world owed me everything it had to offer on a silver platter. I was under the impression that because of my academic success and because I earned a terminal degree, I was in a position of being served. I did not know at the time that the greatest success after obtaining a higher education is being in a position to serve others and to be served. When seeking a higher education, you become responsible and burdened to serve. It comes with the territory. Failing to do so is failing to maximize the gift and opportunity that you have been afforded.

It has taken me some years to get to this point and perspective, which is that the journey to this point has not been easy. There have been many disappointing experiences with friends, colleagues, associates, and even family. Earning a doctorate earns you new "friends" (emphasis intentional) and a few enemies. Some put a target on your back and seek to undermine anything that you do to prove that they are still smarter than, or just as smart as, you are. Others want you to solve all of the world's issues and challenges; after all, you are a doctor, right?

Some people whom you grew up with or whom you have known for years might assume that you feel you are too good or "booshie." In contrast, some do not feel that you have the smarts, intellect, or capabilities to collaborate with them on projects or be a part of their institution.

The homelessness that I experienced, which involved me not really having a home or a place to call my own, led to some lonely and dark days and nights. It would be untruthful to say that the lonely spells that result from an inability or lack of desire to fit in do not still surface, but I have grown more comfortable with the uncomfortable. Some of these rough patches, rejections, and disappointments in professional or academic environments continue to shape my character, outlook, and mission.

Through these circumstances, I started to weed out the elitist mentality and attitude that had silently grown within my heart. These experiences helped me to realize and embrace the responsibility that came with the blessing of higher education. The struggles and challenges have been, and continue to be, a blessing in disguise, regardless of how uncomfortable they sometimes become.

How was I able to overcome these obstacles? Some are still being hurtled and are not completely defeated. However, what keeps me moving forward and continuing to hit milestones, targets, and goals, while having a major impact (sometimes eternal impacts) on others, is a mission that is much larger than I am. Being focused on affecting others in a positive way gives an energy, desire, and strength that cannot entirely be captured in words.

This may be what gave slaves or African Americans living under oppressive Jim Crow laws hope to continue moving forward. I imagine it was the motivation behind Dr. Martin Luther King, Jr.'s drive to write a Letter from a Birmingham Jail or to give such profound and prophetic speeches in the midst of so much hatred and distress. It is likely what inspired Nelson Mandela to pursue the office of the presidency in South Africa, which was a goal to focus on love instead of hate, despite the formal power he possessed and the unimaginable oppression and lost years spent in prison, essentially for the color of his skin.

I imagine it is the drive that allowed Jesus to pray in the Garden of Gethsemane, knowing the fate that was quickly approaching. Crying out to His Heavenly Father while feeling a pressure so intense that He sweated drops of blood. Knowing that He would soon be going to the cross, after living a perfect life free of sin – something no one prior to Him, or no one since, has been able or will ever be able to do. Going to the cross for sins and injustices that He did not commit, taking on the pressure, lies, wickedness, and sin of all people, even having His Heavenly Father turn His back on Him in that moment to fulfill the punishment of sin. Knowing all of this was approaching, He still replied, "Father, if you are willing, remove this cup from me. Nevertheless, not my will, but yours, be done" (Luke 22:42, ESV). Ultimately, I believe what all of these individuals had pushing them to continue on and what does so within myself (please understand that this is not in any shape or form an attempt to compare myself to these aforementioned greats, but instead an attempt to communicate a point) is *faith* and *hope*. I have faith and hope in the belief that continuing to move forward and overcome the obstacles that exist within the world and within my own self will somehow produce positive implications for others.

The Importance of Professional Memberships

Memberships in professional organizations have been critical to my academic achievement. Ultimately, having colleagues, friendships, and opportunities for iron to sharpen iron is critical to almost any endeavor in life. Being a member of professional organizations offers the opportunity to bounce ideas off others; to receive mentorship and guidance from individuals who may have more experience than you; to publish, share, or disseminate thoughts, critiques, research, and opinions; and much more. Professional memberships also provide encouragement, collaboration, and terrific professional networking opportunities. However, professional memberships alone will likely not suffice; you should also have a professional network of friends, associates, and colleagues who may not be a part of a formal organization. Having a strong network of colleagues is a powerful resource. I have a network of African American friends, associates, and colleagues who all have terminal degrees. This network gives me the opportunity to share my experiences in academia or professional practice while listing to their; to collaborate on research, community development, and professional projects; and to continue networking. You should not limit your professional network to only formal organizations or memberships, but you should seek to create a strong network of friends, colleagues, and associates from various backgrounds and disciplines.

Some of the professional organizations that I am a part of are Omega Psi Phi Fraternity, Inc., Project Management Institute, Sigma Iota Epsilon Professional Management Fraternity, Academy of Management, Organizational Development Network, Institute of Behavioral and Applied Management, Fostering Goodwill, *Journal of Negro Education, Journal of Servant Leadership: Theory and Practice, Journal of College Student Research in Education, Journal of African-American Males in Education, United States Journal for Small Business and Entrepreneurship,* Intellectbase, and Mustang Journal.

The Importance of Professional Mentorship

Mentorship is critical, regardless of the context or particular situation. If you can capture and keep a willing, strong, and knowledgeable mentor, your mentor will be a valuable resource and the relationship will provide returns for years to come. Mentorship has influenced my life in many ways. I have already discussed the impact of mentors in my childhood who helped to encourage and propel me into my pursuit of higher education. Mentorship has truly changed my life. I have been blessed to have impactful mentors at several stages in my life, including in my academic and professional pursuits. Professors, mentors, community leaders, pastors, my parents and other family members, managers in organizations, and others have provided strong mentoring that has helped to steer me in the right direction. While obtaining my doctorate, Dr. McCollum was instrumental in helping me to navigate the dissertation process and learn new approaches to mentoring in an academic setting, and he played a significant role in my desire to pursue a career as an educator. Dr. McCollum has remained a consistent friend, colleague, and mentor after my doctoral work was complete by offering insight on strategies regarding careers within academia, opportunities to collaborate on projects, and spiritual guidance. I have also had the opportunity to engage in community development efforts with Dr. McCollum by accompanying him to Haiti on mission trips and by participating in various mentoring program initiatives.

Other mentors such as Dr. Sean Stanley, Dr. Calvin Fogle, Dr. Darrell Burrell, Dr. Emad Rahim, Dr. Maurice Dawson, Dr. Akyna Finch, Dr. David King, and Dr. Charles "Randy" Nichols influenced and mentored me regarding navigating academia, research, and publishing endeavors. These African American academicians and practitioners gave me the opportunity to engage in research projects and helped to coach me through the process. Additionally, they all provided feedback and mentorship regarding academia, provided insight on opportunities, and were always available to offer a positive recommendation to interested parties. These are just some of the examples that show the impact and influence of mentorship on my own academic and professional pursuits.

How I Give Back by Mentoring Others

Due to my own experiences growing, I have been heavily involved in mentoring activities. As I explained earlier, some of my own mentors made sure that I had the opportunity to receive as a mentee and that I understand the value of giving to others by serving as a mentor myself. So beginning in high school, when I mentored inner-city kids and youth in elementary and middle school and ever since, I have been involved in some form of mentorship. I have always had a heart for contributing and giving back to low-income environments, as I have had my own experiences with these types of communities. I believe that our African American communities experience brain drain far too often, where those who do go on to receive particular credentials, higher education, or a particular professional career rarely come back to offer insight, encouragement, or tips that could contribute to others following in our footsteps.

Because of this, I have tried to remain actively involved with mentoring and giving back to others who have fallen on hard times, come from challenging situations, or need a hand up. As a result, I try to stay actively engaged with the homeless community and with at-risk and low-income neighborhoods, and I am working on a strategy to begin engaging more with ex-convicts to offer insight into job training, employment opportunities, and a reduction in recidivism. I also sit on the board of directors for an organization that works with youth who have aged out of the foster care system. These youth often are extremely at risk and lack the training and basic care that most youth who have at least one parent or family guardian present in their lives to rely upon typically receive and often take for granted. It is hard enough to transition into adulthood when you come from a strong, middle-class home but imagine how hard it is for someone to transition into adulthood who has grown up in foster care, has no parents or relatives to rely upon for guidance, mentorship, and ongoing support. The organization that I collaborate with helps to bridge the gap from aging out of foster care to transitioning into adulthood. The nonprofit agency offers services, programs, scholarships, housing, job training, and mentorship so that the youth who receive their services can hopefully pursue higher education or a trade and can have a successful career and life.

Along with working with at-risk or inner-city populations, I teach at multiple universities at the undergraduate and graduate level. As a result, I have many opportunities to serve not only as a professor or educator but also as a mentor. I have chaired or served as a member on many dissertation research committees. As a result, I have had many opportunities to mentor doctoral learners as they pursue their terminal degree. This has been extremely rewarding, as I see this as an opportunity to give back and put even more doctoral degree holders (i.e., social change agents) into communities around the world. One of the universities that I have engaged with for several years is based overseas and has many doctoral learners from distressed, impoverished communities throughout Africa, Europe, and Asia. I have been blessed with the opportunity to mentor individuals from all over the world and to leave my fingerprint on the lives of social change agents and leaders all around the world who can then positively affect the lives of others within their communities and continue to pay it forward. Whether it is grassroots, community development, or international scholarship at the highest degree levels, I have been blessed to contribute to positive social change in the lives of many by leveraging the vehicles of servitude, obedience, and mentorship.

Words of Wisdom for Young Men Seeking to Aspire Higher

I have already provided many recommendations from my own experiences throughout this chapter, but I will provide a few additional tips that have been instrumental in my life and that summarize much of this chapter. If I could sum up my words of wisdom for those that are aspiring higher, I would say, "You cannot and should not do it alone."

First, I would be remiss if I did not say you have to possess a spiritual foundation. For me that spiritual foundation is Faith in Jesus Christ. I am a Follower of Christ, so I subscribe to the thought that we are all born sinners (none of us are perfect) due to the original sin of Adam and Eve. The only way we can achieve eternal forgiveness for our sinful nature is to trust in Jesus Christ, who is the Son of God, incarnated as fully man and fully God, lived a perfect life, but was crucified for our shortcomings and sin, and due to his unjust death (death is a result of sin and Jesus never sinned, so did not deserve death), rose again from the dead 3 days later, solidifying his defeat of sin and death. By believing and trusting in Jesus and what He did for us on the cross, we're promised salvation and forgiveness from our sins and eternal life with God in Heaven (Romans 10:9–10).

This is the belief system that I subscribe to. I have friends, colleagues, and family members who disagree, and we still get along fine. I respect their beliefs and vice versa. I cannot tell you what you must or should believe in, but I certainly think that a spiritual foundation offers benefits while pursuing major life goals and milestones. My Faith has been instrumental in my accomplishments, pursuits, and mission. Without it, I do not believe I would have accomplished these educational and professional milestones.

I also recommend that you surround yourself with the right network. As I have mentioned, finding the right colleagues, friends, associates, and mentors is important. You may not possess this network now or your current pool of contacts may need to be broadened. If this is your current situation, become intentional about achieving this goal. Just be sure to leverage proper etiquette when doing so. It is so common for individuals to reach out when they want something from you, without building a clear case for their need or without offering anything in return. It can become draining and discouraging to have contacts who only seek to take and not give.

Similar to the life lessons I shared from my teenage years, when mentors would often pour into me, but they expected me to, in turn, pour into others, you should seek to discover how you can be a blessing to others, and I can promise you that blessings will find you. If you are pursuing contacts or looking to broaden your network, do not act selfish or thirsty by only looking to benefit from the relationship. Instead, spend as much or more time trying to understand how you may be able to help and contribute to those around you. As a result, potential contacts will be more willing to engage and get to know you while potentially contributing to your pursuits.

Your Mission

I have shared my own experiences throughout this chapter concerning the pursuit of higher education, growth, development, and an academic and professional career. I truly feel blessed! Having an opportunity to reflect in this manner from time to time, as I have done in this chapter, is humbling and is a nice burst of energy to continue moving forward.

Throughout the chapter, I talked a lot about the mission of being a social change agent and the responsibility associated with receiving an education. I hope this was clear. I feel that those of us who are blessed to have the opportunity to pursue higher education always see it as just that – a blessing and responsibility. There are definitely fruits and joy that come with achieving higher learning, and they will manifest in your life.

Obtaining an education can unlock doors and opportunities that would have otherwise remained off limits. The financial rewards, joy, growth as an individual, and much more are simply unreal and unimaginable. Those with a bachelor's degree are estimated to have over $1 million in lifetime earnings in comparison to someone with a high school diploma (Julian, 2012). Those who obtain a doctoral or professional degree are estimated to achieve well over $3 million in a lifetime, which is $2 million more than someone graduating with a bachelor's degree (Julian, 2012). There are true financial rewards from higher education that are worth commending and pursuing. Despite the benefits, power, status, and recognition that come with achieving higher education, there is also a responsibility. Just like the examples I shared from my own experience, like my grandparents, parents, older siblings, mentors during my teenage years, professors, colleagues, and more, when pursuing higher learning, the ultimate aim and goal should not center only on one's self.

If you limit your motivation purely to yourself, then you will run out of energy and purpose and will implode. However, if you keep your eyes on a higher goal, know that you have been commissioned by God to pursue education and use it as a springboard to effect positive social change in your community and maybe even around the world. You will have a fuel and a drive that will keep you moving forward, regardless of what happens. You will have foundational principles, goals, and dreams to revert to during times of calamity, struggle, oppression, injustice, and confusion.

For those of you considering or desiring to pursue higher education, go back to the drawing board, begin reflecting, and ask yourself, "Why do I want to pursue higher learning?" Gauge and test your motives. Determine what you plan to do with your education upon achieving the milestones that you have in mind. How will you effect positive change? What will you do with your degree(s)? Why is it even worth pursuing in the first place? Do some soul searching.

Now to my many brothers, and maybe even sisters, if you have already achieved some sort of higher education, you might want to consider a few more questions. Was your motive right from the very start when you pursued your degree? Did you pursue it only for yourself? If so, how is that working out for you? Are you still motivated to achieve and obtain more? Alternatively, is that emptiness and desire that just cannot seem to be fulfilled no matter what you do, how much you make, or what you buy beginning to wear you down? Maybe you need to see if you are off track or if you started on the wrong track to begin with. Have you started to reach back? Are you making the lives of those around you better? Have you taken the blessing of achieving higher learning and been a blessing to someone else, or is it all about you and yours?

A mission has to be accomplished. Whether you set out with this mission in mind is irrelevant. If you have a platform and influence, which comes with the territory of higher learning, then you have a responsibility…period. Are <u>you</u> going to fulfill <u>your</u> mission?

References

Julian, T. (2012). Work-life earnings by field of degree and occupation for people with a bachelor's degree: 2011. Retrieved from https://www.census.gov/prod/2012pubs/acsbr11-04.pdf

3
Dr. Pettis D. Perry

Professor

Success comes to those who dare to be different.

From Childhood to Higher Education

My parents wanted my brothers and me to attend college because they believed that liberation, freedom, and professional success begin with education and a commitment to lifelong learning. Their efforts produced two sons with doctorates and one who became a highly trained, creative, and brilliant television technician and producer.

In my case, I never doubted that I would go to college – it was only a matter of how long I would be there. Similarly, when my own son was in middle school, he asked me how long he would have to go to college, which warmed my heart and made me chuckle, because he too never questioned going to college. He is now working on his doctorate, which speaks to the importance of education and learning as important family values for those who believe in education as the basis for creating a better life.

My mother had a high school education, while my father had only 15 months of formal education. He was self-taught and one of the most brilliant people I have ever met. They were so well read that they could converse about almost any topic that was brought to the dinner table or a group setting. By the time my father passed away, our home was filled with books, about 3,000 in total. Growing up surrounded by books had a profound impact on me as an adult. I love the smell of books and cannot imagine living without them surrounding me. The thought of a world that is digital and devoid of books is completely foreign to my thinking. Our massive family library became the central focus anytime someone entered our home. In fact, recently, one of my childhood friends spoke about my parents' library some 50 years later during a conversation we were having about our experiences growing up in Altadena, California. The family tradition of sustaining libraries for our children certainly carried over to how I raised my son with my own library containing about 1,000 books. I have reached the point where I have to avoid bookstores because I have a deep-rooted compulsion to buy a book whenever I find myself surrounded by books in a store or library.

My appetite for reading could not be satiated when it came to the science fiction works of Edgar Rice Burroughs, superhero comic books and fables, sports, history, and stories about soldiers in war. My fascination with soldiers in war was tied to the character traits that caused men to do what others refused to do when faced with life-threatening situations and because wars shaped many recorded human events. Little did I know at the time that this attraction would lead to a lifetime fascination with leadership and leader development and would become the foundation for getting my doctorate. My parents were not happy with much of what I read, but they never tried to stop me from reading what I wanted to read. My childhood thirst for reading not only expanded and seeded my imagination about what was possible, but also produced a voracious appetite that continues today for consuming everything of interest.

The fact that my parents were avid historians led me to want to become a historian. In fact, when I began my postsecondary studies, I was a history major specializing in American history. However, about 2 years into my college life, I decided that I wanted to broaden my foundation so that I would not find myself confined to a classroom as a history teacher. Thus, I decided to move toward social science research as my baccalaureate program enabled me to study history while moving me toward other social sciences as well. Because of this shift in paradigms, I began taking sociology, psychology, social psychology, economics, and social science research courses, in addition to history. I then moved into working for human service organizations and committing myself to work in low-income communities to bring about positive social change, which also meant foregoing higher salaries because I wanted to give back to the communities that supported my development. As I moved into my graduate studies, I opted to complete my master's degree in nonprofit administration to strengthen my skills and to demonstrate that what I believed to be true about managing organizations was indeed true. I also hoped that it would demonstrate to those with whom I worked that I was a capable and skilled administrator. To my dismay, it only emphasized that I was becoming more highly trained than my peers and supervisors, which made me an even bigger threat to their leadership in their eyes. After I received my doctorate, I had outgrown the organization in which I had spent most of my career because the organization leaders did not really value education beyond a baccalaureate degree. Thus, I shifted my career to academia, where individuals with doctorates are highly respected and valued and have opportunities for career advancement.

My naiveté regarding academia led me to misjudge how polarized my career would become as I encountered institutional silos with deep and wide chasms resulting from being a practitioner in a world dominated by those without practitioner experience as well as the parochial thinking between the types of doctorates held within a specific school or college. (Colleges house schools that specialize in their degree program offerings. For example, I currently work in the College of Management and Technology, which houses the School of Management and the School of Information Systems and Technology. Each school then houses a variety of degree programs.) As I hold a doctorate of education (EdD), I am often passed over for opportunities by those who hold a doctorate of philosophy (PhD). I sometimes have to laugh because, as a species, we have become so fixated on differences that we can no longer see our similarities, which results in artificial socially constructed in-groups and out-groups comprised of those who are in and those who are out. Artificial social constructs based on stratification practices produce the need to place substantial resources into ensuring that both diversity and inclusion take place within an institution.

Self-talk and Personal Growth

One of the unique things about my parents is that they saw problems, here in the United States and globally, as *class problems* to be solved rather than as *race problems* to be ameliorated, which is an approach that tends to pit races against each other and leaves out large swaths of other marginalized groups based on their demographic stratification. As I have grown older, I have come to appreciate that the class-based perspective was much more encompassing than the perspectives of most of the people I knew, who focused on race as the central point of contention between people here and globally, and therefore shaped the point of attack to bring about meaningful social change through narrowly targeted race-based initiatives. Now living in the 21st century and contemplating its inherent problems, I can see just how correct my parents were in their analysis, and well ahead of their times. Mom and Dad, you were right! It is ever more apparent to me that the problems encountered today continue to be social change issues based in class conflicts rather than race-based conflicts, as proposed publicly by so many and that is consuming so much of our energy. This larger worldview does not negate the more segmented racial divide that exists in so many places, but rather joins it into a larger context that propones social conflicts as problems existing across economic, cultural, and political stratifications rather than as the more demographically defined substratifications such as race, sexual identity, age, socioeconomic status, and gender that are more commonplace today.

Framing the struggle in such a class-based context helped me shape the direction of my lifelong learning practices, education, and professional careers. Practically, this framework caused me to shift my perspective from seeing personalized symptoms to viewing individuals and organizations as parts of whole systems. Shifting my own mental models of how the world is put together helped me to have a better understanding of our individualized connection to our neighborhoods, communities, cities, counties, states, regions, nation, planet, solar system, and universe and the connection of our universe to the entire system of what is now defined as multiverses. That is, seeing our universe as part of many universes. This realization was humbling for sure, but it also helped me to reframe the context for my personalized worldview. As my mental models evolved, so did my thirst for expanding my learning to include such subjects as systems thinking, physics, astronomy, spirituality, and transformative learning. This shift also moved me to develop a better understanding of what Abraham Maslow was talking about when he began discussing self-transcendence just before his death. Since my shift in perspective, I have come to learn that the purpose of life is to transcend self in the service of others, to think about the collective good, and to know that everything I do influences everything else in the multiverse domain. Therefore, what I have done throughout my life, and plan to do for the remainder of my life, was and is important to everything else that has or ever will exist. This profound and thought-provoking realization has since changed the essence of who I am as a human being and how I approach my life's work.

Cornerstones for Achievement

My parents laid the foundation for my success by teaching me commitment to purpose, perseverance, belief in self, a stalwart work ethic, and commitment to excellence. While I was growing up, my parents made every sacrifice to fight for the things they believed in, regardless of the personal costs to themselves or to our family. Such a commitment meant that we often lived without my father being present because he was away on business or we attended meetings and business events with him when he was in town. Sadly, he passed away on one of his trips, so we never had a chance to say goodbye to him. My mother often had to work so we could make ends meet and have enough to eat. From my perspective as a child, it meant that my parents were often not able to attend the events that were most important to me, like when I played baseball, football, and basketball. Nevertheless, they did what they could to attend when possible, and I understood the sacrifices we all had to make. I did not like it, but I did understand it. Although my parents did everything they could to make my life as a child a good thing, someone later in life told me I never really had a childhood. There is a lot of truth in that statement, and it might be why Peter Pan became one of my many heroes and why, to this day, I tell myself that I will never get old as long as my inner child wants to come out and play.

My parents networked with their friends to ensure we experienced cultures from around the world and to make it possible for us to eat foods from every continent, learn folksongs and dances from a wide range of countries, and sing the songs of the working class. As part of our training about *commitment to purpose*, we learned the people's songs, including *John Henry, This Land Is Your Land,* and *Hava Nagila,* and the folk traditions of working-class people. We were also taught that our purpose is to serve the common good and to bring about positive social change by walking picket lines and fighting for workers' rights. Looking back at this time of my life, I realize how impactful those experiences were in shaping me into the person I am today, because everything my parents talked about, they modeled.

They taught me to *persevere* no matter how difficult the task. My father told us myriad stories in which he had to overcome extreme hardships and threats of personal harm to continue his work toward achieving his life purpose. My mother, a second-generation Sicilian, married a man of African descent before it was legal to do so in most states, and consequently she had to endure ostracism by her family and many people in the communities within which we lived. At any time that my father was not working and after he passed away, she had to carry the burden of raising her children and providing for us at great personal cost. She persevered, but I think her efforts shortened her life.

During my early childhood, my mother worked in camp kitchens so that my brothers and I could attend camps that we could not otherwise afford. While growing up, I remember seeing her so exhausted on nearly a daily basis that her eyes drooped, and as soon as she walked into the house, she sat down out of sheer exhaustion. The stories that were read to us as children were stories of hope and perseverance, like *The Little Engine That Could.* Later, *Jonathon Livingston Seagull* became one of my favorite stories because it demonstrates the will to risk and persevere in the face of doubts by those who surround you.

Above all else, my parents taught me that I had to *believe in myself* and my own capacity to achieve my dreams in the face of others who would try to convince me otherwise. My greatest obstacles while growing up came from those who I most trusted and respected. Many of my educational experiences were fraught with teachers, counselors, and coaches who tried to convince me that I was incapable of being successful. Consequently, much of my schooling was not enjoyable because I felt like an outcast. I felt that most of my classmates did not understand me, and I felt my teachers did not want me in their classrooms. Except for only a few teachers, I dreaded going to class and spent much of my time in class daydreaming about something of personal interest or looking forward to recess, gym, and sports. Most of the time I was detached from learning in school, and I saw it simply as unavoidable. I really only cared about maintaining the minimum GPA in order to play sports. The closer I got to the summer recess, the happier I became, and the closer I got to the next school year, the more I started counting the days until the end of it.

Since my parents and their friends were social change agents themselves, I watched the news from a very early age and spent much of my time with adults talking about or listening to subjects of interest to them. Because I had mostly adult interactions, I learned to act like an adult very early in my life, which also meant adults had high expectations that I would take work seriously and work hard when completing my chores and other tasks assigned to me. While growing up, I did not realize that this sort of practice would shape and become my *work ethic* for the rest of my life.

During my early adulthood, I took on assignments that others refused to do so that I could demonstrate my skills and learn new ones. Over the years, I learned to outwork my peers with the belief that I could have the opportunities that they were given even though they were less qualified and did not put in the same effort as me. Time after time, I found others getting promotions and recognitions that I believed I deserved because I outperformed them at every level. Yet, as I looked at myself, I found that I was capable of doing things where others failed because I had built such a solid repertoire of skills. I rarely received recognition for my work or performance and even found proof that others were stealing my work and calling it their own. As a result, I learned to give myself credit for a job well done and refused to become deterred from sustaining my work ethic.

As I rarely received recognition for the things most important to me, periodically I literally patted myself on the back while looking in the mirror to tell myself, "Job well done." I also learned that if I did my job well, others would take credit for it, so I viewed my role as doing such stellar work that I did not leave any fingerprints or footprints, thereby just giving my work to the world. My goal became enjoying the work for the work itself without giving any consideration to recognition from others.

One of my most important lessons was taught to me as a young child when my father told me that *a job worth doing is a job worth doing well*. He laid the foundation for my commitment to excellence. Many years later, when I was an executive leader, a guide who taught me never to sacrifice quality reinforced this further. These two lessons continue to ring in my head because they are engrained as part of the fabric of who I have become over the course of my lifetime.

Mentors, Guides, and Teachers

The role that mentoring plays in the development of initiates and neophytes is long lived. Understanding the meaning and origins of the term requires looking back several thousand years in the historical record. The word *mentor* comes from the classic Greek literary work *The Odyssey*, written by the poet Homer in about the 8th century B.C. *The Odyssey* is the story of Odysseus (known as *Ulysses* in Roman culture), King of Ithaca, husband of Penelope, and father of Telemachus. Begrudgingly, Odysseus joined a war alliance that sailed against Troy during the 10-year Trojan Wars. Knowing that he would be gone for many years, Odysseus asked his loyal friend and counselor Mentor to care for his son Telemachus and his entire household while he was away. Mentor proved to be a trustworthy and loyal counselor and teacher for Telemachus, teaching him the wisdom of the scholars and the ways of a man who would someday rule Ithaca. Today, any person who provides guidance such as Mentor provided Telemachus is called a mentor.

In my experience, mentors have been more willing to act in academia than in other industries with which I am familiar. As a student, I had two mentors. The first was my college defensive-back coach, Coach Chris, who took time during every practice to ask me how I was doing and then worked with me to refine my techniques so I could develop more completely as a football player. Years later, Dr. Lamp, who was my doctoral studies advisor, favorite professor, and department chair, spent many hours teaching me in his classes, talking to me over the course of my program of study about content-specific issues, coaching my growth and development, providing support and encouragement, and even sharing a very personal account about how the previous department chair tried to keep me out of the program. Dr. Lamp supported my application to the doctoral program and later told the previous department chair that I was one of the best students in my program of study. These two mentors made a significant difference during my education and they did so at times when I needed someone to believe in me.

My academic career while on faculty has involved significant periods of personal growth. Dr. Ross, a faculty colleague at San Jose State University, came to my rescue at one of the lowest points in my life when I was encountering what St. John of the Cross, a 16th-century Spanish mystic, called the *dark nights of the soul*. She taught me about having to *ride my demons* and to slay them so that I could move past those things that were holding me back psychologically and spiritually. She also introduced me to transformative learning, which opened a new vista on my understanding of human development and significantly evolved my thinking about leader development. She was a true mentor, guide, and teacher, who, at a critical juncture in my life, showed me the way out of my darkness.

More recently, over the past 8 years with my current employer, that growth centered on surviving a tyrannical supervisor who had become the archetypal adversary – or *demon* – that I have experienced at many points during my lifespan, professionally and otherwise. Dr. Gravett, who shared the same supervisor for several years and thus shared common experiences, became a true mentor and confidant while working with me to survive a horrific supervisor. I was tormented by a supervisor who was psychologically abusive. Over my career, I had experienced exceptionally poor supervision, but nothing comparable to what I experienced under this person. Dr. Gravett is the person I credit for helping me survive the protracted ordeal. Without her support and guidance, I am not sure what I would have done to survive my negative job experiences. In addition, this year, two others with whom I work have offered to help me advance my career. Dr. Schulz is now the assistant to the chief academic officer and Dr. Krysiak was my hiring manager and is once again my supervisor after a nearly 7-year separation that resulted from a reorganization 6 months after I was hired, which led to the supervisor described above. These individuals meet the criteria of being mentors in my professional development, as they each have supported my growth and development.

Outside of my experiences in academia, *guides* and *teachers* (meant loosely here) often appeared rather than *mentors* resulting from formalized relationships or otherwise emerging in structured ways. In this context, *guides* and *teachers* differ from mentors because they illuminate a path by opening a door or they pass along messages rather than actively engage by providing advice and consultation.

Several *guides*, or people with whom I had personal relationships, opened doors for me by either hiring me directly or notifying me of available opportunities. Mr. Dixon launched what became a 30-year career in the YMCA by encouraging me to volunteer, which led to employment. Mr. Lange opened the door for me to become a member of Alpha Phi Alpha Fraternity and joined with me to launch a longstanding consulting career by becoming my consulting partner. Dr. Whitcom, department chair of the Department of Recreation and Leisure Studies at San Jose State University hired me and launched what has thus far been an 18-year career in academia. Dr. Taylor, a former consulting client, opened the door for me to teach at Chapman University and is now a faculty colleague at Walden University. Finally, Mr. DiLorenzi hired me on several occasions when I was without work during a very difficult period of my life. Each of these individuals played key roles in illuminating my path by opening doors and creating opportunities when I needed them.

All of the individuals described above have been instrumental, in one way or another, in my personal and professional growth. They came into my life at key times when I most needed them to be in my life and then disappeared for periods until they reemerged for some other purpose. I found these circumstances aligned well with one of my earlier life lessons from the martial arts. When I was studying martial arts, my *sifu* spoke of the Buddhist proverb, *When the student is ready, the teacher will appear.* I have also found through experience that when the student has evolved, the teacher's job is done and the teacher will disappear. This has certainly been the case in my own life, and I am very thankful for each of the persons who showed up when I needed him or her most.

As far as my own roles as a mentor, guide, and teacher, I have worked with innumerable persons during various parts of my life and continue to work with selected persons who need and want my help. Although I believe that mentoring is a tool that can help people to advance in their careers, and to help young persons without adults in their lives to guide them during difficult times, I believe there are also *guides* who come into our lives at critical times to open doors and create opportunities for us and *teachers* whose purpose is to convey messages and to help us learn some sort of lesson. While mentors tend to be older, or at least more experienced, guides and teachers can be any age. For example, I have learned so many things about life and other ways of being from my son. I learn from the students in my classrooms, those I mentor, and those who have been my clients. In fact, teaching and learning are reciprocal processes. The key is to be open to help and support from wherever it comes. Teaching and guiding others is an unpredictable process that manifests when needed and then goes away, but leaves lasting impressions.

Obstacles or Stepping Stones

Perspective is everything. Whether a glass is half-full or half empty is a matter of perspective. Whether the darkest of clouds forebodes doom and gloom or yields its positive aspect is a matter of perspective. Therefore, whether an obstacle is viewed as an obstruction or as a stepping-stone, is a matter of perspective.

The aging process affords a person with a life well lived the opportunities for daily self-development. Recognizing that personal growth comes from continuous introspection and active engagement with life experiences shapes perspectives in a way that either adds to or detracts from how an individual practices life. As people get older, they have the advantage of time and hindsight about how perspectives have changed over the course of a lifetime resulting from their lived experiences. Those lived experiences can make a person jaded or cynical or they can become the basis for growth and development. The difference in outcomes is contingent upon outlook (attitude) and perspective about how the worldview evolves. My worldview perspective involves seeing life as a spiral rather than as a circle. A spiral connotes growth, whereas a circle is emblematic of redundancy. I choose growth.

Success in any endeavor hinges on perspective, which is a lesson learned when a person lives long enough. As I look back on my own life, my success has been due to my perspective of looking for the positive lessons from even the most negative outcomes. This lesson was first taught to me by my mother, who always looked for the silver lining, and remains in front of me through my son. In fact, my son and I practice searching for the silver lining in all that we do. It is a regular ritual when one of us experiences an outcome we do not like. We perform a simple technique after the anger, frustration, or sadness has subsided by actively looking at what was learned from the experience. For example, in the supervisor experience described above, my silver lining was that I survived the person, which was the first time I had survived a supervisor I did not like. Therefore, although the experience was hurtful, I grew from it by finding ways to assuage my feelings during the period of supervision by learning how to cope with the situation. During the process, I learned new coping skills for working with people I really do not like or respect. One of those coping skills was learning how to live in the moment rather than dwelling on the past or pondering some future state that I could not control. It meant living from moment to moment anytime I had to engage the person. Surviving one moment involved living to survive the next, knowing that at any moment my burden could be lifted, which is exactly what happened when I received notification that the person was no longer my supervisor. Once the situation was resolved, it took a number of months for me to decompress from the abuse. But I made it, and that was the goal.

The best advice I can give to anyone looking at obstacles is to shift perspective in a manner that suits one's personality, yet to move the perspective to see it as some sort of opportunity. This takes practice and has to be done consciously at first, before it becomes a matter of habit over time.

Support Mechanisms

Cultivating support networks is of paramount importance. In my case, this meant separating myself from people who were negative and a drain on my energy, which required making some hard choices to shift my circle of friends with whom I engaged with any sense of regularity. This also meant shifting relationships with family members with whom I did not have good experiences. Selecting good and positive people to have within my circle contributed greatly to increasing the frequency of my positive attitudes and making life for myself much better and healthier.

Transcending my *self* was also an important step in my own development. It caused me to come to grips with what is truly important in my life (e.g., seeing people smile, helping others succeed or feel better, contributing to the welfare of my community) and paid personal dividends such that my life was more fully enriched. This self-transcendence also led me to cultivate a deeper spiritual connection with the forces in the universe that are well beyond my mortal existence.

My fraternal membership and connections within the Alpha Phi Alpha Fraternity have been an important aspect of my support mechanisms. I have also joined other organizations during various periods to enhance my career, but none has come close to my engagement with Alpha Phi Alpha, where I am a life member. Memberships in organizations can become a significant part of a support mechanism.

Higher Education and Personal and Professional Growth

My journey through education did not evolve from an organized plan for my own personal development or as an intentional career path. Rather, it evolved because of circumstance in which there was a weaving of interests, passions, and work opportunities that produced a mosaic that has now defined my career. My education has most certainly produced the basis for exponential personal growth, and it has led to career opportunities, but not through intentional design. This is most likely due to following my passions and my thirst for knowledge through lifelong learning, rather than going to school to get a particular type of degree or job. My jobs are simply my platforms to do my life's work.

As a faculty member and as a mentor, I encourage those with whom I work to follow their passions, to pursue their learning for the sake of learning, and not to worry about GPAs. Now that I have been teaching for nearly 20 years, I have come to realize that those who are pursuing degrees and their GPA often do not learn as much and do not enjoy their journeys as much as those who are following their passions and focusing on how much they are learning while in school. This harkens back to the earlier discussion about perspective. Perspectives also shape focus, and when the focus is on the wrong thing, then learning is not as active as it might otherwise be.

Education also provides the reasoning behind why things occur in real-world experiences by shaping the lenses through which those experiences are viewed. For example, a person educated as a physical therapist sees the world different from a person educated as a computer scientist. In my case, I see the behaviors of people, the dynamics within groups, and the functioning within organizations. So, when contemplating education and training, choose wisely because it will shape your perspectives for how the world appears in very real terms.

My education has enabled me to work for employers in a number of exciting ways, including helping people to grow personally by creating transformative learning experiences for them; working as an executive leader to shape organizations and to test my skills, to coach athletes to maximize their potentialities, and to experience the highs and lows that come along with sports; and transferring technologies by teaching real skills to others. My education has enabled me to broaden my horizons, to travel and experience new places, to meet people I would not otherwise have met, and to continue feeding my insatiable appetite for learning.

Since my education began as a necessary evil that provided a means to play sports, along the way I had to shift my perspective to see the importance of completing my undergraduate degree program as a baseline for obtaining gainful employment, moving into my graduate program to prove to myself and others that I was competent enough to be a manager, shifting perspective to my post-graduate passion for engaging the subject matter, and evolving as a more complete human being with the tools for self-transcendence. Though my education was not planned from the outset as a well-constructed venture, it has become an adventure that has brought me to a place that I could not have predicted. My journey has caused me to make personal sacrifices in terms of time commitments to achieve my purpose, but out of those commitments, I have learned how to use my time more effectively to produce high-end work products that help to make a positive difference in the lives of others and that produce great personal satisfaction. My education journey has also resulted in my developing skills that expanded the number and types of occupations for which I am now qualified.

25 Life Lessons That Have Become My Secrets to Success

The most important thing that I can share about success is to dare to be different. Even twins are different, and your clone would be different from you as well. So, enjoy the differences and embrace all that life has to teach you. Forgive yourself and be good to yourself. There are many people who would like you to be miserable, so do not give them the satisfaction, and do everything you can to enjoy your life. Enjoy the journey and remember that every journey produces lessons that can become secrets to success when travelers pay attention to their surroundings and take the time to stop and *smell the roses*. As a result of the opportunity to write about my life for this book, I have stopped to smell the roses, which is a gift that I did not expect when I sat down to write this manuscript. I now offer some of what I have learned as a list of lessons that have become my secrets to success. I hope they provide some benefit to you.

1. Know that your journey requires commitment to purpose.

2. Have the will to persevere against all odds.

3. Sustain an unwavering belief in self.

4. Develop a stalwart work ethic.

5. Commit to excellence in all that you do.

6. Cultivate an insatiable appetite for learning throughout your entire life.

7. Follow your passion and pursue your education with the right purpose in mind.

8. Know that your education will shape the lenses through which you will see the world.

9. Know from whence you came and give credit to those who helped you get to where you are now.

10. Remember that your education will not be lost and that in the end your path will become clear.

11. Listen intently to those who come into your life, for they have come to convey a message.

12. Walk through doors to explore new adventures when they avail themselves to you.

13. Create a good social support network of people with whom to speak when needed.

14. Seek to identify and embrace your mentors, guides, and teachers.

15. Have faith that your mentors, guides, and teachers will emerge when needed and will disappear when their jobs are done while leaving lasting impressions.

16. Know that trials and tribulations will undoubtedly arise and will become the foundation for teaching you how to become successful.

17. Be humble and treat others as your equals.

18. Live in the moment.

19. Choose your friends and associations wisely, as they will help to define you and will contribute either positively or negatively to your life.

20. Know that all things that have ever existed or will ever exist are connected to each other.

21. Be kind to yourself.

22. Be patient with yourself.

23. Know that you have value and deserve the best that life has to offer.

24. Know that every journey of 10,000 miles begins with the first step and that only your moccasins know the path you have taken to get where you are in this moment.

25. Dare to be different, embrace the journey, and always have fun.

4
Victor Arthur, PhD

Brothers and sisters, I do not consider myself yet to have taken hold of it. But one thing I do: Forgetting what is behind and straining toward what is ahead, [14] I press on toward the goal to win the prize for which God has called me heavenward in Christ Jesus.
—Philippians 3:13-14

What childhood influences sparked your connection to higher education?

As I hold my ProQuest-published dissertation in my hand, marveling at the scholarly work that crowns my academic journey to the highest educational level, my mind goes down memory lane to where it all began. As a child, I took interest in reading, and I still hold dear characters such as Asterix, The Three Musketeers, and Tintin. This childhood influence sparked my connection to higher education. Growing up at Tarkwa, a mining town in Ghana, I had few sources of entertainment. I therefore found joy and fulfillment in reading fiction books. I remember regularly taking the school bus that went by the public library at the town center instead of boarding the bus that would take me home. At the public library, I could immerse myself in various literary works, and I would get lost in the world of fiction stories. The cost, however, was that I had to endure the 1-hour walk home when the library closed for the day. However, the joy of reading made the walk home seem like only a few minutes. I would often rehash the stories in my mind as I walked home, and those reflective moments sowed the seeds of higher education in my young heart. I vowed to learn to write as well as the authors I was reading and developed dreams that would lead me to the corridors of higher education.

At a young age, I practiced putting my thoughts into words. I found a channel to develop my writing skills by composing short stories. In middle school, I wrote a short story titled, "From Frying Pan to Fire" and submitted it for publication in *The Mirror*, a national newspaper in Ghana with national prominence comparable to the *Washington Post* or *New York Times*. To my surprise, my short story was featured in the newspaper. This newspaper only published one short story every Saturday. Therefore, to see my story featured as the story of the week was uplifting. The feeling was indescribable. I ran around showing the story in the newspaper to my friends and neighbors, but most of them had already read it and met me with smiles. I achieved celebrity status in my little town with my story propelling me to the national stage. I made my first trip to Ghana's capital Accra to receive monetary compensation for my short story and to learn more about the publishing industry in Ghana.

In high school, I converted my literary energy into forming a drama group. I mobilized my classmates to join me in forming a drama group to highlight both the joy and the value of literary works. I wrote and directed the play that the group performed, and I led the group to perform both at our high school (Tarkwa Senior High School) and at other prominent centers, including Fijai Senior High School, which was a 4-hour car trip away in the regional capital.

My group was compensated for these performances. We started earning wages to support our education through our own literary initiatives while at the same time enriching our public speaking skills and developing our interest to pursue higher education. The bond that developed among us as drama group members over 20 years ago still holds strong today. A few days ago, some of the members of this drama group, including Theophilus (who now resides in Liverpool, United Kingdom) and Francisca (who now resides in Urban, Alabama), wished me a happy 40th birthday on social media. The journey that started over 20 years ago is ongoing. We were teenagers when we bonded together to grow our love for higher education. Even as adults, with some of us now in our forties, we still share the same value and aspiration for higher education. To us, higher education is an ongoing experience, and we celebrate each milestone as we achieve it.

Describe your educational journey

My educational journey could pass for a fairytale where an unfortunate child met a hero or a good Samaritan who helped to transform a difficult situation into a victorious end (and one might add that they lived happily ever after). I come from a "not so fortunate" background in monetary terms. I started my primary school (Grades 1 through 6) at Tarkwa Roman Catholic Public School. Even though I worked hard to be the best student in my class, the school did not have strong academic standards and students had little to compete for. In sixth grade, I was transferred to Tarkwa Goldfields Preparatory School, which was a top-notch private school. The transfer was made possible through a friend of my uncle who happened to be a teacher at this private school. When I tested for admission to the private school, my test results were not impressive, and I was demoted from sixth grade to fifth grade as the only condition upon which the school would accept me. After crying my heart out, I decided to accept the challenge and moved back a grade in order to attend the school.

My decision paid off, and the private school environment provided me with the competition and motivation I needed to study hard. From the bottom of the class when I first joined the fifth grade at the private school, I worked my way up the academic roster of the class and showed progress each school day. By the end of sixth grade, I had risen to become one of the top students in my class. It was such a great transformation that the teachers showed their admiration by inviting me to join the school's

Commonwealth Essay Competition Writing Team. This was an elite team of students who received special tutoring to compete for the school in regional writing competitions. The instructions and support I received at this stage of my life shaped my academic prowess and placed me on the path to academic success during middle school. I excelled in math, science, and language, and I achieved 12 1's or A's in all 12 subjects that I tested for on the Basic Education Certificate Exams (or BECE, a national exam for students in Ghana at the end of junior high school). To this day, the school has my name engraved at the school as one of the best students in the history of the school. When I visited Ghana recently, I traveled to the school and nearly cried when I saw my name permanently engraved onto a prominent wall as a lasting memorial to current and future students to show them that hard work produces academic excellence. There is truth in the saying that we all are a product of our environment. For me, the rigorous academic environment at the Tarkwa Goldfields Preparatory School groomed me for academic success.

What were the challenges you faced and how did you overcome them?

I faced several challenges during my educational journey. The financial constraints on my family resulted in limited available educational resources. I therefore relied on public resources as much as possible. I frequented the public library to access resources. We had no computers at that time, which was only in the mid-1990s. Thus, when my 4-year-old Rachel takes her iPad or tablet and accesses the ABC Mouse app or my 7-year-old Vanessa takes my iPhone and asks Siri to define a word for her, I look at them and marvel at how blessed the current generation of students are with information being only a few clicks away. During my middle school and high school days, we had to flip through huge dictionaries to find the meaning of words and to build our vocabularies. I am sure my 7-year-old wonders why I want to use a dictionary when Siri could spit out the response quicker!

The financial challenges I faced prevented me from attending a top high school. In Ghana, high schools were not restricted to zip codes but were ranked by academic excellence. Typically, the top high schools were very competitive, and a student needed top scores from the

BECE exams at the junior high school level to attend a high-ranked or top senior high school. Even though I achieved those 12 1's or A's in all my subjects at the BECE and essentially achieved the highest score in the entire nation, I was unable to attend a top senior high school because my family could not afford to pay for the out-of-town trips and the associated tuition fees. Therefore, I had no other choice than to attend Tarkwa Senior High School. Almost all the top students from my junior high school moved over 6 hours out of town to attend top senior high schools such as Achimota High School, Holy Child High School, Mfantsipim High School, and Adisadel High School, but I was left back at Tarkwa Senior High School.

I had dreamed of becoming a medical doctor from an early age. The inability of my family to sponsor me to attend a top senior high school, even though I had top academic scores, made me sad but it did not break me. I resolved to succeed wherever I found myself. I did make one important change, though. I decided to switch my future profession. Instead of pursuing science and becoming a medical doctor, I decided to pursue business subjects and become an accountant. My logic was that Tarkwa Senior High School was not a strong science school and did not have the fully equipped laboratory infrastructure and classroom competition to assist me to succeed as a science student. In my mind, business subjects were easier to study on my own and I felt that I had better chances of exceling in business subjects even at a less prestigious local school. I made a good decision when I chose to switch professions and did not allow my environment to impede my academic progress.

I studied very hard and managed to achieve very good scores on the senior high school national exams, which opened the door for me to be accepted at the University of Ghana (which one could argue is the Harvard of Ghana). I obtained my bachelor of business administration degree with an accounting specialization from the University of Ghana in 2002. I then moved to the University of Maryland and earned my master of science in accounting in 2007. I became a Maryland-licensed Certified Public Accountant in 2008 and went back to the University of Maryland to earn my MBA in 2010. I started working on my PhD program at Walden University in 2013, and in 2017, I had a published dissertation and began calling myself a doctor! What a journey! I spent over a decade studying while working full time. It was a challenging but rewarding journey. I developed scholarly skills and learned valuable lessons along the way, and I became an independent thinker positioned to positively affect society and contribute to effect positive social change.

Ironically, I have become a doctor after all (maybe not a medical doctor, but I am happy that I have become an academic doctor). I am currently the controller heading the finance department of a multi-million-dollar company in Baltimore, Maryland, which is not a bad result from a career change I made as a teenager when I switched from science to business! If we can dream, then our dreams may come true, regardless of the twists and turns that may occur along the way.

What were the successes that confirmed your academic acumen, scholarship, and educational journey?

In an environment laden with limited resources, I pressed on to make the best out of every situation. I produced literary works, passed national exams to enroll at the University of Ghana, and earned a degree. These successes confirmed my academic acumen and taught me that a student has no excuse for poor performance, even when the environment is not so blessed and there are resource limitations all around. I have seen students from very poor backgrounds achieve top academic achievements, and I have seen students from rich families struggle in class. Each student therefore has a responsibility to make the best out of every situation to succeed even in challenging environments.

How did your educational career influence your professional career?

My educational career certainly influenced my professional career. The choice of school for my senior high school education influenced my decision to switch from being a medical doctor to becoming an accountant. It is worth noting that career decisions made at a young age could have lifelong implications and should not be taken lightly. Students need to consider the consequences of such a decision and be sure that they have the best chance at executing the decision.

What are five key attributes/characteristics that you possess as the cornerstone of your achievement?

Perseverance, commitment, dedication, hard work, and focus.

How has earning a higher education influenced your ability to grow and develop personally and professionally?

The attainment of a doctoral degree has provided me with the knowledge and skills needed to achieve my stated academic and professional goals. My passion for teaching was my motivation for pursuing a PhD degree. I pursued a PhD in management with a specialization in finance to empower me to teach and advance in corporate leadership. Since fall 2009, I have worked part time as a teaching assistant tutoring a graduate accounting class at the University of Maryland University College. Higher education has equipped me to both contribute to knowledge in academic settings and disseminate knowledge in professional environments.

What were some of the obstacles you have had to face post earning a higher degree?

The major obstacle I have faced has been meeting the high expectation that society now expects from me as a doctoral degree holder, especially when it comes to disseminating my research work.

How were you able to overcome the obstacles?

I have overcome this obstacle by remaining calm and committing to be myself. This has allowed me to deliver on expected goals and move the agenda forward.

How has membership in professional organizations contributed to your academic achievement?

Being a member of the American Institute of Certified Public Accountants makes available to me current professional resources, including the *Journal of Accountancy*, to help me to stay informed.

How important has professional mentorship been in your ability to move onward and upward, both academically and professionally?

Mentorship has been instrumental in shaping me academically and professionally. I have looked up to role models such as Greg Hemingway, former director of accounting at Bravo Health, who I worked for as a senior accountant. He endorsed my CPA license and inspired me to move higher in the corporate accounting world.

I have also been motivated by the self-actualization work of Abraham Maslow, which involved examining theories that provided a spectrum of ideas on using creative capacities that leaders could draw from to accomplish maximum use of their creative skills and provide satisfaction of self-worth in their pursuit of relevant goals in life. According to Abrami (2011), Maslow did not limit creativity to professionals. Rather, he attributed creativity to all people who were able to use the few skills and resources they had to produce good results.

What is your association with mentorship? How have you mentored others to move onward and upward?

Students come to me for counseling and coaching. I receive referrals from parents who want their children to hear and learn from my academic and professional successes. I feel humbled at such requests and do the best I can to provide valuable information that can help to make the path to success achievable.

What are some words of wisdom you would like to share with young men who are aspiring higher personally and professionally?

I would advise young men to persevere and work hard to achieve their dreams. They should not allow the challenges within their environments to deter them, but they should focus on the prize and go get it.

What was your step-by-step strategy/approach to achieving excellence in higher education (tools, systems, processes, tips)?

My strategy has been to evaluate available resources and make the best out of them. Whether in a traditional classroom setting or an online environment, I assess available resources in terms of what is needed to succeed and I work to use these resources to achieve my goals.

What were some key lessons that you learned about yourself that demonstrates personal growth?

From my years of experience in both the academic and the professional worlds, I have learned that success is achievable if a person invests the appropriate effort into achieving it. I have learned not to allow challenges to dissuade me. If I could come out of a limited-resource environment to earn a bachelor's degree, two master's degrees, a CPA license, and a PhD degree while working full time at the postgraduate level with growing family responsibilities, then anyone can achieve higher education and become successful academically and professionally by investing the appropriate effort into the process.

How are you using your educational achievement to change the world? How has your territory been enlarged?

I am using my educational achievement to change my society one person at a time. Whether it is encouraging a student to study hard to pass a test or guiding a young person to make career decisions, I provide valuable information that can guide people to make informed decisions.

From a very young age, I aspired to position myself in a way that would enable me to contribute to society. I knew then, even as I know now, that education is an important tool to achieve this goal. From elementary school through high school and then to college, I studied hard, knowing that the skills and experiences that I was acquiring were relevant in equipping me to become a better contributor to society through teaching. I wanted to be a part of change implementation in my community (Stragalas, 2010). The opportunity to acquire the knowledge and skills that would enable me to teach at the highest level of academia in order to contribute to society was my primary motivation for pursing a PhD degree.

My academic goals were as follows:

1. Complete my PhD degree within 5 years
2. Achieve self-fulfillment by obtaining a PhD degree
3. Contribute to society by sharing knowledge acquired from my PhD degree

My professional goals are as follows:

1. Teach as a faculty member of a reputable university
2. Advance in corporate management within a large company
3. Become a consultant of my own company

According to the *Essential Guide to Online Learning* (2003), school is a laboratory for life, and working with other students is good preparation for future collaboration. My personal and professional goals are founded on using educational opportunities that will equip me to work with other people to make me a better person and build an improved society.

The contribution of practitioner-scholars to society is rewarding (Bartunek, 2008). I plan to use the knowledge and skills acquired through higher education to contribute to society through teaching and corporate leadership. I plan to impact individuals and society one day at a time.

References

Abrami, L. (2011). The concept of a personal calling: In the works of several psychoanalysts and philosophers. *Journal of Spirituality in Mental Health, 13*, 207–219. doi:10.1080/19349637.2011.593409

Bartunek, J. M. (2008). You're an organization development practitioner-scholar: Can you contribute to organization theory? *Organization Management Journal, 5*, 6–16. doi:10.1057/omj.2008.3

Essential guide to online learning. (2013). Baltimore, MD: Laureate International Universities.

Sellars, M. (1974). One day at a time. Retrieved from https://alchetron.com/Marilyn-Sellars

Stragalas, N. (2010). Improving change implementation. *OD Practitioner, 42*, 31–38. Retrieved from https://pdfs.semanticscholar.org

Walden University. (n.d.). About us-Walden Online University. Retrieved from http://www.waldenu.edu/About-Us.htm

5
Dr. Calvin Nobles

According to research, 6% of Black men ranging in age from 18 to 64 are incarcerated. More alarming is that 34% of working-age Black men who are not incarcerated are ex-offenders. When compared to other men, Black men have higher statistics for living in poverty, being unemployed, and earning lower wages. Worst of all is that only 17% of Black men have a college degree (African American Population Report).

Humble Beginnings

My motivation to pursue a college education was based on my humble beginnings in Mt. Vernon, Georgia, which is a small rural town. Some people find it hard to believe that I come from such humble beginnings where I was raised in a single-wide trailer with my siblings. As a young boy, my life consisted of playing sports and working. My mother was very strict and a disciplinarian, especially when it came to our grades. Studying was mandatory and came second to our daily chores. My mother believed it was important to teach children responsibility and accountability at an early age. In our household, any grades below a B were unacceptable and often resulted in disciplinarian action or punishment. As the product of a broken home, we faced many financial hardships, and I made a promise to myself to pull myself out of poverty and never to endure such hardships again. I started working at the age of 12 because of my family's financial difficulties. Most of the jobs were odd jobs with meager wages, but I needed the income. From that time forward, I always had a job to help support the family. Working as a preteen taught me that education was the key to escaping poverty. As an adult, I gained a greater appreciation for my humble beginnings because it shaped my perspective, instilled unprecedented levels of tenacity, and serves as a reminder to keep achieving.

Leveraging Athletic or Inner Instinct

Sports were a major part of my upbringing, and they taught me teamwork, devotion, and strategy development and blessed me with an inculcated competitive nature to win that serves as an internal fire. Playing sports also provided an outlet to avoid the pain in my life as a young boy and adolescent. I was ashamed of my hardships and often tried to hide those difficulties to avoid being ridiculed by others. Sports taught me many life lessons, especially playing high school football and baseball. As a football player, my team won several regional championships, which served as my first taste of winning. These sports instincts continue to surface in my life when I am pursuing goals because the obstacles and the process become the opponent and my internal fire coupled with mental prowess provides the ability to strategize and conquer the goals. Your goals must be supported by realistic time frames, resources, and devotion. I have seen many young men and women detach from their dreams due to the level of perseverance and determination needed to conquer those goals. You should also seek sponsorship and mentorship to ensure you stay on course and for positive reinforcement. As a mentor of doctoral students, I observe my mentees' frustration while undertaking the laborious process of pursuing a doctoral degree. I suggest they focus on the quality of their work rather than on the milestones and timelines for completing the degree, because everyone is different. For those who do not play sports, being involved in some organization or extracurricular activity that motivates or provides a positive outlook can serve as an igniter. Although you should never forget where you are from, it is more important to focus on where you are going.

Learn to Dream

I always had a fascination with the military as a young boy. And as a teenager, I would often dream about life without poverty. Shortly after high school and after realizing that I needed a college education, I enlisted in the U.S. Navy with the purpose of earning a college degree. The military provided the necessities and much more because I was a natural fit in the Navy. Sometimes you have to endure hardship to pursue goals. An advantage of serving honorably in the Navy is the ability to capitalize on the educational opportunities. I served around the world and at every duty station I quickly enrolled in college courses and earned a bachelor of science degree within 6 years of joining the Navy. Over the course of my naval career, I earned several graduate degrees and a doctoral degree. My success in the military is indicative of dreaming and believing. Many successful people are dreamers because they are able to envision success and put together a plan to pursue their goals. Regardless of the challenges, you need to find and achieve success. Never stop dreaming!

Be the One!

Pursuing a college degree was part of a personal desire to place distance between my new rewarding career in the Navy and my humble beginnings. My family lacked a long lineage of college graduates; in fact, only one family member had graduated from college. Mr. Eddie Wright, an iconic pillar of our small community, confided in me about the training and educational opportunities in the military. Mr. Wright was acutely aware of my family's financial plight and realized that serving in the military could potentially serve as a ladder to greater success. At Mr. Wright's behest, and accompanied by my own personal determination, I engaged on an education frenzy shortly after reporting to my first duty station and completed one class after another. The military instilled two things in me: discipline and confidence. After failing the first semester of 12th-grade English, I knew that getting through college would be an uphill struggle, but I was dedicated to the cause. As a result, I passed English 101 and 102 with flying colors. The pursuit of a college degree was not just a personal goal but served to inspire other family members to do likewise and to break the pattern. Educational goals can sometimes serve a dual purpose by inspiring others to follow a similar path. At times, you have to be the one who shoulders the family's problems by being a beacon of light and carving a path toward success.

Formal education is imperative to driving toward success, and even though some people can become financially secure without formal education, most cannot. Through a formal education, I was ingrained with an affinity for reading that still exists today. By engaging in extensive reading, you are in fact self-educating. Many Black pioneers such as Frederick Douglass, Booker T. Washington, and Benjamin Banneker were trailblazers who leveraged self-education. However, formal education alone is not enough to enter the annals of success. As aspiring businessmen, scientists, doctors, lawyers, entrepreneurs, politicians, clergymen, authors, educators, and community pillars, you need to capitalize on formal education, self-education, and memberships in professional social organizations. Each plays a vital role in shaping, educating, and exposing you to many unknowns. Professional social organizations function as networking and sponsorship catalysts to provide privileged information for professional and personal growth. Do not underestimate the significance of professional social organizations. Leverage social media to research potential social organizations that align to your profession and seek membership. However, membership alone lacks fertilization; therefore, as a member of a professional social organization, you should explore opportunities to serve, engage, and learn – never stop learning. No one is going to hand you a playbook to navigate the bowels of success; consequently, you have to be the one to take the initiative and seek opportunities.

You Have to Be Comfortable Being Uncomfortable!

At times, taking the initiative will rattle nerves and make you nauseated. However, as an ascending leader, you have to fight through the difficult feelings and find the will power to succeed in the most vulnerable times. It is imperative to be resilient and to be comfortable being uncomfortable. No two days are alike; be prepared to be uncomfortable. When seizing the initiative and leaning forward, some will discourage, belittle, and sabotage your willingness; nonetheless, you should stay focused and control your nerves. For example, your mentors and sponsors should not be a mirror image of you. Diversify your pool of mentors and sponsors, even it means reaching out to someone of a different race, sex, religion, culture, or belief. It is natural for most people to reach out to those who they relate to, but it is not easy to contact an individual, group, or business with different views. Most of my mentors are not a reflection of me; some are female, white, or Islamic or have a different perspective. The key is to learn to diversify your network portfolio and seek opportunities to grow and develop from intellectual discourse with mentors and sponsors. One must be comfortable being uncomfortable to capitalize on different opportunities that might be foreign or a bit outside of your strengths. Accepting being uncomfortable will provide the inner desire to pursue bigger goals. In an academic environment, especially in graduate-level programs and beyond or in a professional setting, you might be the only minority, so cherish the opportunity to represent and look forward to working with classmates who offer different perspectives.

Establish a Positive Support System

While on the journey to success, others, including family members, might not understand your quest. Do not expect everyone's help and support while you are achieving benchmarks along the journey, because some will not understand the meaning of your accomplishments. Therefore, how can someone provide support when that person does not understand the situation? Along the journey of success, you will lose contact with family, friends, acquaintances, neighbors, and co-workers. You should understand that for others who have not pursued analogous endeavors, your journey is incomprehensible, which is why they will not understand the devotion and discipline required to climb the ladder of success. It is not that these people do not care, but other people do not have the same passion for your success. Surround yourself with like-minded individuals who are tracking in the same direction. Building a positive support system is crucial given that it provides an outlet during setbacks, during lulls, and when the goals seem unachievable. With the ascendancy of social media, many like-minded trailblazers are pursuing similar goals; you should also be an inspiration to the next brothers to the left and right of you. Cherish the network and be sure to reciprocate to others in your network. When your goals seem impossible, rely on your network to lift your spirits and remind you that there will be pain and joy when climbing the ladder of success. Remember after the journey there are no ticker-tape parades, but just the network of people who provided support along your journey. Be gracious and thankful enough to provide each with recognition for serving as a footstool so you can rise to the top.

Climbing the Ladder

Achieving success is a gradual process that requires devotion, discipline, and the intellectual and mental prowess to withstand roadblocks and setbacks. When climbing a ladder, it is hard to ascend without taking steps, and the same principles apply when seeking success. For example, when pursuing a college degree, a litany of distractions can prevent one from succeeding. You should remain tenaciously focused and devoted to achieving a college degree. It is imperative to earn your college degree, even if you are 40 years old when you finish. As men, we are pillars and living examples in our communities; therefore, we are the beacons of light and providers of hope for each other – and especially for our women and children. Once you are ascending the ladder, the goal is to keep moving upward and never descend from your progress. Be prepared to face controversy, hardships, failures, and drama along the way, but the primary objective is never to give up because you are a beacon of hope. While serving in the military, I faced many obstacles and challenges. Some depleted my energy but not my focus and tenacity to accomplish whatever goals I had set. This is why your network is your confidant. Whether pursuing a college education, working toward a promotion, or starting a business, the principal goal is never to stop climbing. However, it is possible to slow down, refocus, recharge, and continue moving toward the top of the ladder. In life, everyone gets a ladder; however, some people never decide to climb the ladder, while others make climbing the ladder a lifelong goal. While climbing the ladder, it is vital to cheer for other brothers who are ascending and encourage those brothers who are yet to start the journey to wait no more – the ladder awaits them. Being successful starts with achieving small victories, building on your successes, and creating a recipe for success. One victory is not enough to consider yourself a winner, though it might be admirable; you therefore need to establish a record of small victories that will become your steps to a bigger triumph. By establishing a history of winning, you will develop the hunger and the drive for more successes.

Everyone's ladder is different, and so is everyone's journey to success; there is no standardized template for success. A ladder is a metaphorical symbol to illustrate the successful navigation to a goal. Although your journey might consist of stepping from one ladder to the next, the same principles of success apply – never descend and never give up.

Finding Your Wind

Along the doctoral journey, sleep is not a priority, as the dissertation process is unforgiving and unforgettable. Most people who have completed a doctorate will speak to the tireless and relentless efforts required to complete the degree. Embarking on a path to success requires incredible drive and the ability to push yourself beyond personal limits. In short, you need exceptional stamina when pursuing goals, especially educational goals. It is imperative to find your wind so you can tackle the late nights, frustrations, and group assignments. Your stamina is chemically enabled by the tenacity to fight and the mental fortitude to achieve one milestone after the next. I often hear people making excuses for why it is too difficult to attain a personal or professional goal, and I cringe because it highlights their lack of stamina. Find your wind by any means necessary. As a researcher, I am naturally motivated by drafting ideas on paper and driving concepts to codified substance. You have to find positive aspects of the endeavors to provide the wind to reach success. Every person is motivated differently; therefore, a person must discover what things are motivating and stimulating to increase stamina. Finding your wind goes beyond a single episode; in fact, it is a way of life, and you have to know how to leverage your chemical repositories to provide stamina. Stamina is an attribute that empowers a person to exceed normal levels of energy. Endurance is important because it will provide the horsepower to propel you up the ladder of success and the ability to loiter without depleting all your energy. Stamina is the attribute that allows successful people to grind on a continuous basis with very little or no sleep at all. Find your wind and develop the endurance to continue climbing the ladder of success.

Taking Losing Off the Table

Earlier I alluded to being ashamed of my humble beginnings. Today, whenever I am pursuing my goals, I reflect on my humble beginnings as a motivation to climb the ladder of success when the only option is achieving the goal. My favorite saying is *losing is not an option*, because eliminating losing as an option compels people to seek a different choice. Many people are derailed from the ladder of success because losing remains an option that offers an early out or becomes the path of least resistance. In the wilderness, smaller animals often fight larger animals and win, and this is known as the survival of the fittest. Sometimes you have to challenge yourself to determine your internal fight. In extremis, humans are capable of demonstrating and achieving amazing things due to chemical stimulation that provides incredible strength. Some supernatural motivation occurs because losing is not an accepted option, which increases the willingness to fight. While pursuing educational and career goals, you have to develop the inclination to graduate and eradicate losing from the list of options. Reflect and think about how to remove all the different types of losing from your life. In the movie *Rudy*, the title character demonstrated unequivocal zeal to play football at Notre Dame – even though the odds stacked against him were overwhelming. Rudy removed losing from the plan and endured brutal beatings on the scout team. Sometimes in life, you have to outmaneuver physical and mental obstructions to stay on the ladder of success by demonstrating zeal to win because losing is not an option. In other words, be Rudy – do not let obstacles impede you from achieving your goals and remember losing is not a viable option.

Establish a Relationship With a Higher Calling

I would be remiss not to mention my belief and grounding in a higher calling. God's graciousness and innumerable blessings influenced the direction of my life. I accepted Christ as a teenager, and he shows me favor. Thank God daily, and let him determine the course for your life. Your spiritual being is a requirement for success. As you encounter difficulty while pursuing personal and professional goals, remember to confide in a higher calling. It is only a matter of time before you encounter trouble, but you have a readily available remedy in God. I use my God card on a consistent basis because he is the only one who can provide the comfort and protection I need. I recommend maintaining a strong belief in a higher calling to serve.

Conclusion

You have an incredible life ahead of you. You are a pillar of the community and should cherish the countless opportunities available. Tirelessly pursue your education to position yourself for victory and continue to accomplish small victories to build a portfolio of triumph. Never give up, and remember losing is not an option.

6
Chernoh Wurie, PhD

Professor

I have learned that people will forget what you said, people will forget what you did, but people will never forget how you made them feel.

—Dr. Maya Angelou

Higher education has always been my goal and motivation in life. To achieve this goal, two primary reasons fueled this passion. First, as an African native born in a small town in Sierra Leone, education was my top priority. Second, both my parents worked tirelessly to secure government-assisted higher education endeavors in Sierra Leone. Education in Africa is not a top priority for many; however, with two parents who demonstrated to me that obtaining higher education was possible, I had to make this a priority and a goal of mine. In addition, as I was born and mostly raised in Africa, I highly value the benefits higher education has to offer. I will expound further on my story. Currently, I am a full-time criminal justice faculty member at Virginia Commonwealth University, a former 10-year veteran police officer of an elite police force, and a former crime scene investigator. I currently reside in the greater Richmond, Virginia, area with my best friend and wife Jennifer and our two lovely children – Jamessin and Eliza.

My story is unique. As mentioned above, I was born and mostly raised in Africa, specifically Free Town, Sierra Leone. Sierra Leone is a third-world country that has many natural resources, such as diamonds, gold, and other fine minerals. These minerals ended up in the wrong hands, and as a result, a civil war erupted. My family and I fled the war-torn country and migrated to the Republic of Guinea. We stayed in Guinea for about 6 months and were able to obtain visitor visas to come to the United States.

Upon migrating to the United States at age 17 years, and after seeing so much hurt and political unrest in my country, I made it a point of duty not to waste my life and to use the opportunities presented to me in the U.S. My educational journey was somewhat discombobulated, diverse, and filled with culture shock. In 1997, I was in the midst of taking my GCE O-level examinations, equivalent to a high school diploma, when the war broke in my city Free Town. Upon being forced to flee the war-torn city, I was not able to finish my exams. During my 6-month stay in Guinea, I did not attend school, but the educational drive was haunting me every day. I felt that I had to do more with my life. I kept my mind engaged and read detective novels and other crime-solving-related novels. I was fascinated with crime solving, and this passion later led me to my career as a police officer and a crime scene investigator. Upon migrating to the U.S., I enrolled at C. D. Hylton High School as a junior. However, based on differences in the educational system where I was from, I was demoted down one grade to a sophomore in high school. Thus, although I was taking my final exams to start pursuing my college career in Sierra Leone, I ended up a grade or two behind in high school in the U.S. This decision infuriated me, but I took comfort in the fact that I was in the U.S., the land of opportunity, and I felt I should be grateful and make the best of it. My early high school years were awkward. I was enrolled in a school in 1997 in which the African American population was about 1% and about 2% of the population were other, mixed, or non-White – everyone else was White. My brother and I were the only African students in the school.

Some challenges and hurdles in high school were the language, culture, acceptance, food, communication, and so forth. I had the preconceived notion that African American students would be more accepting to my brother and me and would befriend us; however, the complete opposite happened. I was completely shunned and ignored by the African American students. I was even ridiculed and asked questions such as, "Did you used to live in trees?" "Did you have any clothes or did you wear clothes where you are from?" This enraged me, and I lashed out by getting into fights and defending my culture and beliefs. In the midst of this, I was not doing very well in my classes because American English and British English, which is primarily used in my country, were somewhat different in spelling and pronunciation. With my grades declining and after having several meetings with the guidance counselors due to my fights, I was spiraling downward quickly. I was tempted to seek out other students who were shunned and ignored. I was drawn to the particular crowd that had a coping mechanism for dealing with constantly being ignored, which involved turning to drugs and other mechanisms that provided a recreational high. Even though I knew this crowd would accept me, I stayed away from them as much as possible. What motivated me not to stray away from my learning was my self-motivation. I always knew what I wanted to be when I grow up. As I mentioned earlier, I have always had a passion for law enforcement, and I would ask myself what would happen if I got involved in drugs and other criminal activities and behaviors and how would this affect my career choice. At the age of 17, I researched the requirements to become a police officer. In addition, there was a school resource officer assigned to my high school. His name was Officer Marvin Scott. Although he did not know it, he strongly influenced me in taking the right path, staying out of trouble, and becoming a police officer later in my life. He would hold periodic talks in classes, the library, and the cafeteria. I would attend each talk and would speak with him afterwards. I learned a lot from Officer Scott. He was very patient and understanding. Even though my accent was very hard to understand, he would make sure he reiterated every point made to me in our conversations.

Another channel that assisted me in dealing with the struggles in high school was sports. I ran track back in Africa, and I was good. I enrolled in my high school track and field program, and I did very well in my events. I made many friends and felt somewhat accepted in my high school. The moral of dealing with my high school hurdles was twofold: I conquered my struggles in my early educational path through self-motivation and by excelling in something I was good at. These two primary focal points assisted me throughout my adulthood and my higher education endeavors. Upon completing high school in 1999, I enrolled in a local community college (Northern Virginia Community College), where I spent 2 years, raised my GPA, and successfully completed my associate's in administration of justice (cum laude). I then proceeded to Radford University, where I completed my bachelor's in criminal justice in 2004. After finishing my bachelors, I joined an elite police department in 2005 and separated in good standing in July 2015 in order to transition into teaching higher education. During my tenure as a police officer, I also completed my master's (2009) and doctoral studies (2012) in public policy and administration with a concentration in public safety administration. In 2013, I published my first book, *Impact: A Compilation of Positive Police Encounters.*

My educational career greatly influenced my professional career. Five key attributes that contributed to my success in both my educational and my career achievements are *knowing* what I wanted to do, having a *positive attitude*, building *networking/mentoring* relationships, and being my *own advocate and critic*. Knowing what I wanted to do as a professional career paved the path for me. Being fascinated with police and detective work, it was easy to declare my major in criminal justice and pursued it throughout my educational journey.

Knowing what I wanted to be eliminated any wasting of time in college. Having the passion for police work fueled my drive. I can recall sitting in the front of my Organized Crime class, which was taught by Dr. James O'Connor (retired FBI special agent). He was one of my role models and motivators, and he had a certain style and way of teaching. He would begin by telling us stories of his years as an agent. He would then relate his experiences to the class materials; thus, I was able to understand and relate to the course materials much clearly. I now use his style of teaching in my own classes by relying somewhat on my professional experience to support my practical and theoretical knowledge to deliver my lectures.

Having a positive attitude has also influenced my success in achieving my career and educational goals. Life has a strange way of throwing obstacles in our way, and I have always had the mind-set that an obstacle is just another way of making us grow and deal with life. Having a positive attitude got me out of a lot difficult and strenuous situations, especially while pursuing my dream career and my higher education goals. To become a police officer, there are a lot of higher standard requirements to meet (U.S. citizen, good credit, good physical health, good moral and ethical standing, good driving record, no drug or alcohol violations, clean background check, psychologically balanced, etc.). While pursuing my dream career, I did not meet at least one or two of these requirements, but through my positive attitude and persistence, I was able to demonstrate my character to my employer, and as a result, my employer was able to work with me in achieving my dream career. Anything is possible if one puts forth the effort, and this was my motto while pursuing a career as a police officer. While pursuing my doctoral degree, there were times when the work would get difficult and my initial response was to quit and resort to just having a master's degree. For example, while attempting to collect data from a protected population, disclosing to the potential participants that I was a police officer deterred them from participating. Having a positive attitude ultimately guided my participants to being willing to participate. They did not trust the police and did not want anything to do with police officers, but with my positive attitude, I was able to convince them that my study was beneficial and that I would portray their unheard voices.

Networking/mentoring is a key ingredient in success. The connections I made throughout my career and on my educational journey were personally developed and have played a remarkable role in my life, and I am grateful for these connections. I applied for several teaching positions both online and in class after completing my doctoral degree, but the basic online application process did not yield any job opportunities. Therefore, I decided to take it upon myself to make connections with department deans and chairs. I arranged meetings with them and ultimately I was able to acquire part-time teaching opportunities for several prestigious colleges and universities.

Similarly, I would not have completed my doctoral program successfully without the help of mentoring. Sometime late in the 2009–2010 school year, I was on my way to my first residency in Florida. I was sitting quietly in the terminal waiting for my flight when I was approached by a very nice gentleman. I was filled with anxiety and nervousness, as this was my first residency, and I did not know what to expect. This gentleman was dressed casually (sweats if I remember correctly), and we started talking about the flight and our destinations. He then introduced himself as Dr. Walter McCollum (aka Dr. Mac) and told me that he was heading to the same residency. He also mentioned that he was one of the program organizers and had completed his doctoral program in a different discipline than mine. He was very helpful; he made me feel like I could handle my program, even though we are from two different disciplines; and he was very helpful. He also gave me his contact information, and we have remained good friends ever since. He took me under his wing and guided me throughout my entire dissertation process. The fact that we are from two different programs did not stop him from assisting me. He persisted in ensuring I was doing well, and he was more helpful than my dissertation committee members were. I am forever grateful for his friendship, love, caring, and dedication to my success. I have mirrored his behavior, committed to mentoring several mentees, and have taken them under my wing at my current institution. Dr. Mac challenged me and changed my life. I have vowed to do the same to other young and upcoming students.

Being my own advocate and critic was one of the most difficult strategies I developed for myself in reference to my success. The saying that we are our worst critics is accurate in my situation. Even when I was a small boy growing up in Africa, I was an overachiever. I was and still am very hard on myself with regard to accomplishing my goals and dreams. I have traced my entire childhood and have concluded that this was entrenched in me by my father. One distinct example occurred when I was in Class 6, which is equivalent to Grade 8 or 9 in the U.S. The students were assessed with various assessment tools in our classes, and at the end of each quarter, we would receive our scores ranked in order of positions from the first to the last person in the class. I worked my hardest to maintain a position in the first 10 out of 40 or 50 students. One quarter

I placed third in my assessment. I was very excited, and I shared the news with my dad. He was also thrilled, but he also reminded me that two more students did better than I did. I truly believe that his statement motivated me to want to be the best at what I do. I know my father was proud of my accomplishments and of me; however, it was difficult for him to show this because he wanted me to be the best and the first in everything I undertook. I placed first in a few instances and made him and myself very proud. I have taken my father's attitude and have let it guide me throughout my entire career, educational choices, and initiatives. However, while this concept can be motivating and ambitious, it also has its disadvantages. It made me feel less of myself whenever I was not selected for a promotion or did not do well on an assessment, and I would go so far as to think that my efforts toward the endeavor were in vain. Over the years, I have learned to cope with the fact that a person cannot excel in everything, and sometimes even when a person excels, he or she cannot be selected due to other factors at play. Another example was my sergeant promotional exam in 2014 with the police department. The first time I took the promotional exam in 2012, I was unprepared and not ready for it, and I placed 40th out of 50 applicants. This score was detrimental to me, as I was very hard on myself. In 2014, I thoroughly prepared myself and I scored third out of 44 participants. Even though I was elated by my outcome, I was filled with mixed emotions. I also asked myself why I did not score first, as I knew each participant was separated by just a fraction of a point. The point to this story was that even though we can be our toughest critics, we can also learn to channel this energy into something positive and learn from our mistakes to be the best we can be.

A very good friend of mine once asked me, "How are you using your educational achievements to change the world?" I did not have to ponder much to answer this question. It is simple: I have seen many walks of life and have experienced many situations from emigrating from Africa to the U.S., experiencing culture shock in high school, becoming a police officer, and obtaining my doctoral degree, and I owe it all to one major character trait: perseverance. Even though the road may seem short and unpassable at times, perseverance has always been my motivational factor in carrying forward. Referring back to the question of how my educational achievement is changing the world, I would say it is changing the world immensely; in my current faculty position at a prestigious university, I am the conduit of our future generation. Having a background in law enforcement also shaped my patience in interacting with various population sets. As Dr. Mac did for me during my doctoral studies, I have copied this same mentality as a criminal justice faculty member, and I have taken on mentoring and counseling 40–80 students from various disciplines across the United States within various schools.

Words of wisdom that have guided me through my educational and professional journey are being my own advocate and being the change that I so dearly desire in various walks of life. For instance, I was having a spirited conversation with the students in one of my classes in the midst of all the police shootings during the summer of 2016. There were about seven students in the class, including both Black students and White students. The conversation became very serious once we started discussing the issue of unarmed African American males becoming the victims of these shootings. One of my outspoken Black students mentioned that she was from the District of Columbia and that she was in a constant state of fear that her father, brother, or boyfriend would be a victim of such a tragedy, as it seemed to be a pandemic that was plaguing young African American males in the United States. I did not interrupt her. I listened to her carefully and so did the entire class. After she finished making her point concisely, I asked her one question, "If you are so displeased with the criminal justice system, then why are you a criminal justice student?" She responded, "Professor Wurie, I want to be the change, I want to successfully complete my degree and work my way through the criminal justice system and make the change from the inside." Her words echoed with me for months, and even today, I have used her statements in several panel discussions. She is right. One thing I want to pass on to our young African American males is for them to be their own advocate and become the change. One cannot sit and expect someone else to make that change for them. They have to become that change and effect the change from the inside. I am thankful for being selected to participate in this excellent endeavor, and I will continue to be my own advocate and continue to effect changes within my organization as well. My institution is currently lacking minority faculty members, and I have made it a personal goal to push for hiring qualified diversity candidates within my department. Due to my efforts, I was elected unanimously to be the chair of the school's equity and diversity committee. The endeavor of bringing in qualified diversity candidates is a never-ending process, as they are needed in order to have a meaningful ratio of minority faculty members and minority students. These relationships are imperative because of peer mentors and teacher–student mentoring relationships. I am actively working on expanding our department in this endeavor.

Last and most important, I am thankful for my family – my wife and best friend Jennifer and my children. They are my light and guiding agents. They are there to bring happiness and love. Without them, I would not have much motivation and purpose in life. They are the driving force behind everything I do. God and family comes first, and everything else comes second.

7
Dr. Brian Grizzell

Educator

I grew up in a village. And not to produce any segue into the ancient proverb of how it takes a village to raise a child, but in many ways it was my surroundings that nurtured me into education. My neighborhood was filled with educators – my elementary and junior high school principals lived around the corner from my family's home. My grandmother and all of my aunts and uncles were educators, so education was not just an option for me; rather, it was an expectation of my responsibility to uphold what I was nurtured to be. My grandmother told me at the age of 5 that "an education was the only thing a person could not take" from me. I owned that.

My mom was a city girl who went to Tougaloo College but did not graduate. She got a job with U.S. Postal Service and retired after a 32-year career. She worked her way up to a high-ranked GS employee. My father was a country boy who completed high school and went to work. He was one of the first Black police officers for Jackson Police Department and did construction on the side to provide for our family. I am the youngest of six children, and four of my siblings went to college, so from a young age, I admired people like my mother and father, who were hard workers and never let their circumstances define them negatively, and people who knew that life would have vicissitudes, but hard work was needed to create any lasting change.

Abraham Lincoln was an American politician and lawyer who served as the 16th president of the United States from March 1861 until his assassination in April 1865. He found his way into history books as being the premier politician advocating for democracy and individual freedoms afforded to us by our God-given rights. I once read a quote from Lincoln that resonated with me and serves as a good rationale for my educational influences: "Things may come to those who wait, but only the things left by those who hustle." Now, many may think that the word *hustle* is something that can be negative: *hustler* on the street, dating "the *hustler*" from the neighborhood; connotation has its way of debunking the value of words. However, to hustle is to propel one's self forward; to be a go-getter; and to be hungry enough to work hard enough to make sure you eat, your family eats, and have more than enough left over. The things that my grandmother told me at the age of 5 allowed me to learn at a young age that in order for me to get what I needed, I had to hustle, and I found my way to becoming more educated as a result.

Many do not know the pitfalls that Lincoln endured. Yes, he was responsible for freeing millions from bondage, but he had to come to an agreement that took years to get to the point where equality is a right and not a luxury – much like me. I grew up attending Jackson State University (JSU) football games, and from attending these sporting events and hanging out with my older siblings and cousins on campus, I knew that I wanted more and more. It took years of exposure to the benefits of education, and the benefit in sticking to something to achieve greatness, for me to realize what my life needed to become. I was also able to witness how some did not understand the value that education can bring to one's life. See, Lincoln freed slaves on paper, but mental servitude lasted for decades after. Only recently have Black males been privy to the information that others have known for centuries: education brings power.

I was a high achiever and began my educational experience expected to only be the best. I went to public school from kindergarten to 12th grade. I loved school. I was active in choir and band. I took honors courses and continuously made high honor roll. I missed the National Honor Society by 1/10th of a point; I was devastated because to me, I was supposed to maintain greatness; however, my parents told me to suck up the loss. My journey was not always going to be smooth, so I was made to understand that taking one on the chin is sometimes the best way to build character and much-needed fortitude.

This was some of the best advice for me when it came to taking standardized tests. Even though I knew I was smart, I could never really get a feel for the tests. Therefore, standardized testing was a struggle for me. I made a 20 on the ACT, but needed a 21 for an honors college scholarship; I just could not get it after three tries. However, I was still ranked 44 out of 344 students in my high school senior class and was awarded a scholarship to JSU with the Sonic Boom of the South, JSU's premier marching band. However, I chose to go Mississippi State University (MSU) first, which proved to be a huge mistake. In college, I made several honors societies, but when my father passed away in 1994, I could not regain any standing at the predominately White institution, and I failed tremendously. MSU lacked the support I needed.

T. S. Eliot once wrote, "People to whom nothing has ever happened cannot understand the unimportance of events." Trying to be the best, not making it into the honor society – things like that no longer felt momentous. Losing my father was devastating enough at that time for me to look back at some of the things to which I gave so much importance. It allowed me to put myself into perspective and to see that what was going to benefit me was to position myself where I was going to have the support to be great, not just be positioned at an institution that seems prestigious. No disrespect to MSU or any other institution intended! I was leaning on reputation rather than my own emotional uplift on which education is contingent.

In January 1996, I transferred to JSU, and I finished on time despite losing credits. I even hit a 3.5 GPA my last semester (taking major courses and 21 hours). I loved college; I cried at graduation because my mom *made* me graduate! I still laugh at that.

The journey was not without struggle. I failed the English proficiency exam. I did not try because it made no sense to me. I still find no rationale that says a college student should take a writing test before he or she graduates. Education is not just about writing; education is about critical thinking. Well, I guess in hindsight that I could have tried a little. Nevertheless, I made A's and B's in most of my English classes.

However, my freshman composition professor told me I could not write. He also never helped me to improve my writing. Thus, I took it upon myself to become a better writer – that was motivation enough. To date, I have 50 publications, three graduate degrees (including a doctorate), and will soon have a second doctorate. My life is great, and I can credit the hustle instilled within me to my parents and grandparents for the greatness I have achieved and for the greatness I have yet to achieve. The advice I would give others, and even my younger self, is to understand your own place in this world so that no person's negative words can dissuade you. Negative energy is only stifling to the weak; it can also be a motivation to continue to become better. The cornerstone of my achievement can be summed up in five attributes: maturity, deference, status, perceived power, and enlightenment.

Stephen Covey popularized the concept of beginning with the end in mind. It is believed that if a person wants to propel him or herself into a position of greatness and power, he or she must begin with that vision in mind. Initially, I wanted to be a lawyer, so I majored in English. After my professor discouraged me, I did some self-reflecting and realized that I am better in areas that are more mathematical and scientific. Therefore, I changed my major and chose the major that had the fewest English requirements.

I first went to accounting, but I did not even finish intermediate accounting before I changed my major again. The professors were horrible and impersonal. I enjoyed the material, but I knew this was still not a good fit for who I wanted to become. I changed to management and that bored me to death! I wanted to work with money, numbers, businesses, etc., but the management material was not for me. I changed to finance and it was heaven! It was the perfect balance for me. I was able to learn about managing money and other fiscal requirements, and I was able to see how all of this could fit into my future. The material was not easy by any means, but it also helped to have four line brothers to take classes with. It was hard! I learned a lot though. The professors were amazing and willing to help. I felt at home. I learned that you do not always find the perfect fit on the first try. It took me two colleges and five different majors to find my niche. I persisted, and I ultimately found a major that I loved.

Audemus jura nostra defendere is a Latin phrase also used as the state motto of Alabama. *We dare to defend our rights* – referring to individuals who understand their fundamental rights, who are daring enough to defend their position to have and acquire said rights. Abraham Lincoln freed slaves, thus ending a practice that built the Americas. However, defending our position as an important component of society has been a struggle for Black males since we were *given* the rights to be a free person. Often in the literature we are seen as the archetypal Black Brute, a dark-pigmented savage who knows nothing but how to take, steal, and harass. Alternatively, we are seen as the dimwitted jokester whose slapstick approach to life is only for amusement and belittlement. It has been my goal to take that stereotype and use it as motivation to do more. Higher education was my way of not just propelling myself forward, but also dispelling any myths about Black men and our propensity toward savagery or mental slowness.

However, I almost quit my PhD program because I was extremely intimidated by the success and skill sets of my cohort members. I came into the program bright-eyed and ready to grow, but everyone else seemed to have it together. I felt inadequate; all the others seemed to know what they were doing! Nevertheless, I remained realistic and humble. I sought ways to be a part of my cohort, but not to assimilate. See, I had my own mission in my mind at all times. Even though the enemy initially tried to make me see myself as less or inferior, I soon realized that I had something that others did not: the determination to be greater than my circumstances. I did not come with a chip on my shoulder thinking I was better than anyone else because I was accepted into a terminal degree program. Rather, I saw this as an opportunity to continue with what my parents and grandparents instilled within me about what can never be taken away from me.

I persevered and surrounded myself with the right people, and I was the only one to earn my PhD out of my cohort. It seems surprising, but they all lacked the hustle, the determination, and the persistence to become better. Higher education allowed me to align myself with the right people. I learned how to sort out those who did not mean me any good or those who feigned a supposed rank. I also learned that the ones who are loud about having their lives together usually do not, and I could not allow someone else's words or rank to intimidate me. My battle was for me; it was mine and mine alone. My HBCU experience forced me to grow up quickly and forced me to figure out how to solve problems on my own. I was able to use what my parents taught me and become a better man.

Research has shown that rural communities will soon be a thing of the past. By 2030, the bulk of the world will be urban, much like what occurred during the boom of the industrial revolution, and small towns and villages will be replaced with machinery and skyscrapers that transform the skyline. However, as time progresses, what it means to be urban progresses too. For a long time, if a person was urban, he or she had proclivities toward African Americanism, a cultural demarcation of Blackness. American culture is now leaning toward becoming more urban and abandoning the small-town mentality. But what about the villages that raise young Black boys to become catalysts of change as they grow into Black men? Research also shows that as time has progressed, so has the definition of a nuclear family. Where a household was once considered a father, mother, and their children has extended to include a mother and her children, a father and a mother alone, grandparents and children, and even children alone. The sustainability of the notion that it takes a village must now evolve into other modes of propelling Black men. It is therefore important for professional organizations to become an essential component in the lives of young Black men so that the goal of success can be seen through mentors and others. We will still need a village, but the village will look a little different as time progresses.

Membership in professional associations is a necessary investment for Black males. The tacit knowledge gained at conferences/meetings and hiring opportunities are insurmountable. Because I am a part of organizations such as the Academy of Management, the National Association of Chief Diversity Officers, and the American Education Research Association, I have been privy to many opportunities that align with my personal mission.

These memberships have allowed me to move onward and upward and especially came in handy when learning to how to be published in peer-reviewed journals and navigate academic conferences. Again, aligning myself with the right people proved to be a beneficial part of my own growth as a professional. However, the journey is not without obstacles. Even though education is something that cannot be taken away from me or from any other academic, I still have to eat, and employment has been a huge obstacle, especially in the south, where people are both overeducated and inexperienced, are overeducated for the minimal qualifications, or do not have the desired pedigree. Education is a place where learning constantly happens, including learning about oneself. I've had to hustle my way into positions, not in a negative way of course, but I have aligned myself with the right people who understood my determination and that my experience on paper pales in comparison to what I can do when presented with the opportunity.

Virtus tentamine gaudet is another Latin saying that translates to *Strength rejoices in challenges*. Challenges and obstacles are a part of life. They are as inescapable as gravity; we will always be at the mercy of them, but just as humanity has found ways to defy gravity, so can Black males defy obstacles. The obstacles create strength. Physical strength is great; with all due respect, our nation was built because of Black males and our physical strength, but having mental fortitude is as equally as important, and that obstacle can only be conquered through education.

However, it sometimes takes an outside force to intervene. *Vir prudens non contra ventum ming* loosely translates to *A wise man knows not to piss in the wind*. It's not possible to know it all; sometimes we all need a little incentive from others to allow us to realize our own capabilities and maybe to help us to realize that we are doing things that are useless and not worth the energy. Mentorships have always been important to me because paying it forward is the only way many can receive what I did. I pay it forward as much as possible. Just like others helped me to be published and learn the ropes, I have reached back and helped countless others. I am also a dissertation coach and have assisted dozens in completing that final document that stands between them and their terminal degree. I allow my mentees to understand that it is okay to ask for help and ask many questions. Learn and listen, align yourself with the right people, and purposefully build your support mechanisms.

I learned that my path to success is an individual journey. What may have worked for others may or may not work for me, and that is okay. I had to concentrate on what I need and want, and do what is necessary. I had many failures, but I learned from each one and continued to grow. Through all of my education, I am an educator, too. I took what was instilled within me, that education could not be taken from me, and I sow that seed within my own students. They may not have the foundation that I had, but I make sure that they understand that their journey is for them and them alone, and once actualized, it is a life that will be fulfilled. The only way we all can create positive social change is to stay focused on the goals that we want and not on what others have defined for us. Learn all you can, because being able to defend your viewpoint with viable information is gold in many circumstances and will help you shine. As my grandmother allowed me to realize many years ago, my education is mine, my journey is mine, and my life is one that is fulfilled because I chose to seek a higher understanding.

8
Dr. Ben Magee

Business Owner

A number of things influenced my childhood growing up in the Deep South (Gulfport, Mississippi). I was fortunate to be raised by a village, which is something missing in today's communities and society in general. We not only had our parents, but we also had our teachers at school and elders in our communities (the barbershop). My father was not present in my life growing up. He actually left my mother before anyone knew if I was a girl or a boy. The task of raising three children (at the time) was left to my mother. My mother was not formally trained and after my father left, my mother, who had a high school education at best, found work as a janitor for most of my formative years and later as a short-order and truck-stop cook. My mother fueled my thirst for learning and instilled in me a high work ethic and a sense of pride in whatever you do. She would tell me, "If you are a janitor, be the best janitor you can be." You can only do your best and no one else's best, but you must hold yourself accountable. She was not book smart, but she was very wise, and she did a great job of teaching life lessons.

My mom would tell me that one of the toughest things in the South was being Black, and the second toughest thing was being a Black boy or man. I would always see the nicely dressed White men downtown and wonder what they did and where they were going. Even though my mom was not college educated, she would always push me and my siblings academically to be more than just average. I knew at an early age that I wanted to do more with my life and I did not want to be a janitor or a cook, even though those are noble professions. I wanted to find a way to reach as many people and help as many as I could. The turning point for me came very early, at 9 years old. I remember watching a clip on the news of President John F. Kennedy giving his inaugural address (although I am not sure why it was on), and I remember the last few lines as if it was yesterday: "ask not what your country can do for you, but what you can do for your country." Little did I know that statement would resonate with me for the next 40-odd years and drive me to achieve extraordinary academic achievements.

I was able to use my athletic abilities to earn a football scholarship to the University of Alabama. I was excited and knew this was an opportunity to get a great education and play a sport that I loved. I always remembered my "why" – why I was pushing myself and doing what I was doing. First, I wanted to provide for my family, both present and future, and I knew that I could do that through education and football. What I did not expect was being injured at such an early age. I graduated from high school at the age of 16 and the best thing that happened to me was being injured. My injury was not career ending, but more so enlightening and life changing. It made me take a step back and realize that my desire to leave the game was much stronger than my desire to stay. I felt that God had a higher purpose for my life, and it did not include football, at least not playing at that time. Not bad insight for a 19-year-old kid! After my short football career ended, I remembered the excerpt that I had watched of President Kennedy some 10 years before, and it hit me – service to many – and with that, I decided to join the military.

My career began as a 2-year enlistment in the Army to earn the GI Bill so that I could continue my education. That 2-year enlistment turned into a 16-year military career (active duty, reserves, and National Guard) with tours in Europe, Asia, the Old Guard, and as sentinel of the Tomb of the Unknown Soldier, which was the highlight of my career. With the help of Uncle Sam and the support of my wife Marie, I was able to pursue and earn several undergraduate degrees, an MBA, dual master's degrees, and a dual doctorate. The more I learned, the more I grew, both academically and professionally. Education did not change the color of my skin, but it did change my lifestyle and way of life. I was not born into privilege, but through my education, hard work, and determination, my children were and so will their children be.

The more that I learned and educated myself, both formally and through life experiences, the more I grew in my professional career. I was able to advance in the workplace and receive more positions of leadership and authority. I was able to influence others through my education. I was actually the first male in my family to graduate from college and subsequently earn my doctorate. Pursuing higher education opened my mind to the possibilities that I can do anything that I put my mind to and that we are only products and victims of our environment if we choose to be. I always had a purpose for the educational path that I chose and I wanted my education to mean something to me first. My education pushed me to be more and do more and ultimately influenced me to think outside the box and to begin creating my own boxes and then to think outside of them. I do not think I would have started any businesses if it were not for the influence of higher education.

The following are the five characteristics or attributes to my success or achievement:

1. Build your life around a purpose ("why") and never stop dreaming. If you do not have a plan for your life, then you are not living and you are simply existing.
2. Take chances and do not be afraid to fail, because the by-product of failure is success!
3. Find a way to serve the many. Leave your mark; when you encounter new people, leave them better

than they were before they met you. Make a difference.
4. Have an attitude; there is nothing wrong with an attitude.
5. Challenge yourself daily and never settle for average.
6. Share your gifts; be generous.

A great deal of respect is garnered when one earns degrees in higher education. I think the more that I learned and educated myself, the more I was able to grow and develop personally and professionally. Earning higher education degrees has enhanced my ability to influence others as well. Higher education has become an obsession for me. It is a thirst that I cannot and frankly will not quench. It has influenced my way of thinking and the ways I cope with situations in life and in business. My higher education has afforded opportunities to speak, train, and educate other professionals, which has helped and is continuing to help me to grow mentally, intellectually, and financially.

I would say that I have had more mental obstacles than physical obstacles to overcome. I was an entrepreneur long before I decided to advance my education beyond a bachelor's degree. One of the biggest obstacles that I faced was finding a way to leverage my advanced degree to further my business practice and build my personal and corporate brand. I think obtaining the degrees was easy. My motivation and my "why" was not really rooted in advancing my corporate career, as my small business was beginning to grow. We often spend too much time working for our degrees, and we do not let our degrees work for us. I overcame the mental obstacles by finding a way to leverage my advanced education. Some of the mental obstacles were the constant questions from family and friends, "Why are you going back to school, you already have a successful business, you are making good money" and on and on. If was definitely more mental for me.

I was able to overcome those mental blocks or obstacles by staying true to why I was doing what I was doing. I am a person and a man of principle, and I believe in leading by example. I am a father of four impressionable children and young adults and two of those children are young Black men. I am on constant alert because they are always watching, observing, and learning from me. I was able to use my advanced education as a validation of sorts. I was always told that Black men had to work twice as hard for twice as less! So do we ever overcome the obstacles? I really viewed the obstacles as a series of peaks and valleys, where the peaks represent proficiency and the valleys represent learning.

Membership in professional organizations has played a key role in my academic achievement and in my career. When I was working for Booz Allen and Hamilton back in early 2000, I was encouraged to join the company's local chapter of Toastmasters. After one of the meetings, I was speaking with a group of colleagues, and they told me about the university cohort program that Booz had with Johns Hopkins University, whereby the professors would teach the program from the local offices of Booz. The company would pay for the program as long as the student maintained a B or above average. The program was still relatively new and the first cohort had already begun, so I waited until the next semester to join the second cohort. I completed the 3-year program and earned a dual master's degree in telecommunications and information management systems from the Carey School of Business & Education. If I had not been convinced to join that cohort, I do not think I would have had the opportunity to earn a master's degree from such a prestigious university. That is one example of how professional memberships have contributed to my academic achievement. I then continued to pursue my doctorate from Johns Hopkins as well as a doctorate in management information systems from Kennedy-Western University.

I maintain memberships in several organizations:

- Omega Psi Phi Fraternity, Inc.
- NAACP Silver Life Member
- MENSA International Organization
- American College of Forensic Examiners Institute
- Disabled American Veteran Association
- United States Old Guard Associations
- Institute of Electrical and Electronics Engineers – Advisory Board

I have been very fortunate to have great mentors in my life, both professionally and academically. I have also been able to reconnect with several of my college professors and high school teachers though social media. It has been great to connect with individuals that I feel helped to shape my life and tell them, "Thank you!"

My professional career began after college in the military where I was trained as an infantry soldier, Army ranger, and later as a sentinel at the Tomb of the Unknown Soldier. I definitely had mentors in the military, as that is a major part of one's success. I think a person limits his or her success by not having mentors. Booz Allen stressed the need to have subordinate, peer, and senior mentors.

I started my career outside of the military in the financial industry, and I was fortunate to have a great mentor whom I met by chance. I worked for a company named Quotron Systems, Inc. and the company was a wholly owned subsidiary of Citicorp and later Citigroup after they merged with Travelers. To make a long story short, the CEO of Quotron was John S. Reed, who was also co-chair and co-CEO of Citigroup. Mr. Reed went on to be the chairman of the New York Stock Exchange. I commuted to New York daily for over 3 years. I worked at 99 Wall Street and on occasion had the opportunity to have coffee with Mr. Reed. I was able to gain knowledge that would become very valuable, and I am still benefiting from that knowledge today. I have been able to share my knowledge of financial literacy and fiduciary responsibility with my protégés and mentees. I have also been able to leverage that relationship to add a form of credibility to what I do and represent.

I have used my experience running successful companies and organizations to mentor small businesses and start-up companies. I created a small business consortium in 2003 as a way for small businesses to collaborate on developing business through contracting opportunities. I led the consortium for about 9 years and realized that we could do more, so in 2012 we formed the minority-owned coalition. We also incorporated a community outreach program that grew into a nonprofit organization in May 2013 called the Minority Owned Business Coalition, Inc. (MOBC). MOBC is a registered 501(c)(3) nonprofit organization founded as a small business consortium to provide financial assistance, endowments, scholarships, and mentorship to companies, underserved communities, and youth.

MOBC was conceived under the auspices of filling a void in the small business community by creating an organization that would build a small business consortium consisting of companies with various backgrounds, skill sets, and levels of expertise. These companies would not only support their corporate missions through MOBC partnerships and teaming, but also served communities and other charitable organizations and missions.

MOBC members include a consortium of small, medium, and large businesses; schools and universities; and banks. We created the Young MOBC Program (YMP) that is a mentor- and protégé-centric group comprised of students, young adults, and entrepreneurs ranging from ages 16 to 29. The YMP was designed to create an atmosphere where members have the opportunity to interact and collaborate with business owners and government stakeholders. Young MOBCs are encouraged to takes risks and collaborate to solve problems. The MOBC Small Business Consortium facilitates the YMP by helping YMP participants prepare for adulthood and be successful in all of their endeavors by promoting and fostering financial literacy and by building

- Life skills
- Lifestyle development
- Interpersonal skills
- Business and career success

Find your "why," build your foundation upon it, carry it with you, and use it in everything that you do. What is motivating you to get up every morning? Never quench your thirst for learning. If it were easy, everyone would do it, because if it does not challenge you, it will not change you. Hold yourself accountable, and do not blame anyone for your failures; that is why they are called *your* failures. Be passionate about what you do. I have not used an alarm clock in over 30 years because my passion wakes me up! Find something you are passionate about and be the best at it. Be disruptive, and do not be afraid to take the road less traveled because you will never have to worry about traffic jams.

I do not think there is a holy grail to the process of higher education, but I do believe you need to have a strategy. If that is a step-by-step process, I do not know. Sometimes it felt like I was shooting from the hip or building it as I went along. My tools were the strong support system of my wife and immediate family. I did not listen to the nay-sayers, and as much as I wanted to share my progress with others outside of my family, I refrained, as sometimes those outside of your circle can be distractions. I was able to build a 10-step recipe for success:

1. Build your life around a purpose (why) and never stop dreaming. If you do not have a plan for your

life, then you are not living and you are simply existing.
2. Take chances and do not be afraid to fail, because the by-product of failure is success! Have an unrelenting appetite for success!
3. Find a way to serve the many, as service to many equals success.
4. Leave your mark; when you encounter new people, leave them better than they were before they met you.
5. Make a difference. Stop waiting for someone to make a change; be the change that you want to see in the world; a fire always begins with a spark – be that spark.
6. Have an attitude; there is nothing wrong with an attitude.
7. Challenge yourself daily and never settle for average; always remember to hold yourself accountable.
8. Share your gifts, be generous, and use your education to educate others.
9. Learn something new every day.
10. Be kind; it is the easiest thing in the world to do, but seldom accomplished.

My life is far from over, or at least I hope it is; I am still learning every day. I have learned how to speak life into whatever it is that I want to accomplish. I have come from wearing the same clothes every day to wearing designer and tailored clothes. Education is the key. I have challenged myself to read a book a week, and the more I read, the more I grow. I was able to awaken some of the things that I learned in the military and continued challenging myself and pushing myself beyond the point of mental and physical drain to experience a sense of enlightenment that cannot be explained, only experienced. The following are some of the key lessons learned through my journey, this life's journey, thus far:

- What is your "why"?
- You don't know how far you can go until you push yourself to your breaking point and then push more
- We are limitless in our capability and capacity to learn
- Never quench your thirst and desire to be better than you were the day before
- Your success or failure is in your hands, and there is no one to blame but you
- In order to start, you first have to begin

- When you think you have lost your way, remember "why"

I have used my formal and life education to build a successful business and to change the lives of thousands of people and hundreds of families. My "why" has grown exponentially! I founded Bull Run Capital Investments, LLC (BRC), a private equity and venture capital company, in 2010. BRC currently has 12 companies under management. I am using my educational achievements to continue to build businesses and to help others build businesses and change lives.

Financial literacy has become my life's mission. BRC has invested in a sports complex, and through professional relationships leveraged through higher education, we are going to begin building sports complexes around the country. I am also a life coach, business coach and consultant, business mentor, youth leader, and inspirational speaker. I am using social media to market and promote my brand. I think it is important to brand yourself. I am also the president and CEO of an IT and cyber-security firm that has a national footprint and supports clients in over 20 locations across the country.

Educational achievement has had a profound impact on my life and the life of my family. Higher education has afforded me the opportunity to build a legacy that will benefit not just my family but generations of people! The journey has not been easy; nothing in life worth having ever comes easy. I have sacrificed vacations, trips, and even high-paying jobs, but I learned a long time ago that in order to go up, you have to be willing to give up (things). So to you I say, onward and upward BLACK MAN!

9
John C. Lofton, III, PhD

President, John Lofton & Associates

The greatest adventure you can take is to live the life of your dreams.

I grew up in a scholarly family. My grandfather was a high school principal in Mobile, Alabama, during the civil rights movement. My great grandfather worked with Dr. Martin Luther King. This is a proud family fact and the photos I have of them together are a treasured family heirloom. During my childhood, learning was something we did because having the right to do so was something that many had been beaten for and some actually died for. It is challenging for me to understand why most people do not realize the power in continual learning. Being stuck in the rut of today was never an option for me because I saw the world literally change before my eyes and concluded that it would continue to change. Therefore, I persevered and continued to run short races until I was able to walk across the stage with my doctorate.

My grandfather was a principal to most but a philosopher to me, even if he was not speaking directly to me. He once shared something with a visitor in his home that has remained with me to this day. He said that philosophy is the sum total of everything we know. Part of that equation includes what we think is valuable and the things we actually use. Thus, to move beyond what we use and value, I chose higher education to gain different perspectives and to challenge what I knew. I listened to information I agreed with and information that was counter to my beliefs.

The first thing I will say is that the journey was long! As a military member engaged in higher education, there were deployments, family moves, classes that had to be dropped, and deaths of friends and family. The one thing that became my anchor was that I had always noticed that successful people maintained a positive focus on life no matter what circumstance. There are enough challenges and people that will try to stop your desire for advancement, but I focused on my successes instead of dwelling on failures. The failures actually became the lessons that helped plan the steps that would get me closer to my goals. The deployments, moves, and dropped classes were the prices I paid to defend the freedoms of those in this country. The deaths that I had to cope with still torment me today because of the constant "what ifs" and the times I said "I only wish." Things happen for a reason, and if a goal is important enough to you, any adversity you face can become your advantage if you allow it to push you to grow. If you fall, it forces you to get better, so why avoid the fall? It is not how fast you start, but how consistent you remain. The successes that have confirmed my academic acumen, scholarship, and educational journey continue to grow by the day. I earned my PhD with Distinction. I have the honor of being associated with the men you are reading about in the book. I have the important task of mentoring the next wave of great minds. The list goes on.

My educational career has influenced my professional career by providing opportunities. All anyone can ever truly ask for is an opportunity. An opportunity provides the canvas for you to shine. Picasso said, "Others have seen what is and asked why. I have seen what could be and asked why not." My educational career moved me from going through the day taking on one obstacle after the next to allowing me to stop wondering what if. I now have the opportunity to determine "how can" and ask "why not." Thanks to my education, the barriers have been torn down and I am now able to challenge my limits. It is not that I could not have done it before, it is that I now have a more receptive audience when it comes to the ideas I share.

For me, vision is the foundation of who I am as a person. Being a visionary allows me keep hope and possibility in front of me and those with whom I interact. Ambition also plays a critical part in who I am, because it helps provide strength to the environment I operate in. When people experience ambition, they know that we deeply believe in where we are heading and why. Dedication becomes vital when you shape your environment based on a vision and ambition. Having the ambition to cast a vision is one thing, but when you inspire others with a plan, you have the dedication to follow it through to reality.

Character is often defined as who you are when no one is looking. It means purposefully pursuing the elements that will help you grow regardless of whether they get immediate attention. Our character becomes essential in how effectively we influence others. For that reason, we have to maintain a level of honesty because people are watching, studying, mimicking, following, or criticizing every move we make. If people do not see honesty in our lives, we have limited influence.

Earning a higher education has influenced my ability to grow and develop personally and professionally because I am now able to appreciate perspectives other than my personal views. I like to say that I am a waiter who waits tables. I am now able to be a servant because I stay with and help those in need. There is truly nothing like knowing your calling. To be the one serving and not the one seated reminds me that I have reached a point where I can help those who are less fortunate. From the top, the blinders are blown off by the wind so that we no longer have tunnel vision.

The biggest obstacle I had was myself. I had to figure out what to do next. I had no real plan; I only knew I wanted my doctorate. Obstacles can be massive in scale, such as war, terror, disease, and death. Although I have experienced each, with the exception of disease, most obstacles we experience are less drastic, but they can still disrupt our lives, such as hate, pride, jealousy, and selfishness. These obstacles can interfere with the accomplishments we can achieve. Any obstacle that I experience is nothing more than a challenge. The challenge acts as a filter to block out anyone who may not truly want the prize at the end of the challenge. Obstacles make you work for what you want. There are two options: stop or persevere toward what is meant to be.

Imagine what could happen if everyone read things that were positive or enlightening at least 30 minutes a day. Our body would become fueled by positivity, not the negativity that consumes the world. Medical doctors advocate the importance of a well-balanced diet, but you should remember to feed your mind a healthy diet of information from your craft. That is most easily accomplished through professional organizations. Membership associates you with like-minded individuals and keeps you informed on the most current topics of your field. I have memberships with Project Transition USA, Council of College and Military Educators, Accreditation Council for Business Schools and Programs, Society of Nonprofits, Association of Nonprofits, Institute for Operations Research and the Management Sciences, and the Logistics Officer Association.

My mentors were the reason I made it through my doctoral program. Dr. Best and Dr. Henderson in particular were some of the best mentors and friends I could have asked for. They actually sat me down and taught me the process for writing, reading, and analyzing at the doctoral level. I am now a professional with a best-selling book and mentees I am now helping through their programs. True mentors of this world are like ship lights in a stormy night. They shine a ray of hope. They give you a signal that allows you to focus on the correct target. The most important thing is that when you are lost, they choose to be there with you and not watch from the sideline.

I am currently an active mentor of five doctoral candidates. I have previously mentored two candidates to completion of their degree. Professionally, I mentor with each contact I have with people. When you are known as doctor, you become one who is frequently searched for. As a mentor, I have grown to understand that the only way we can truly see is when we navigate through challenges. Not many have become smarter simply by sitting on the sideline. We grow through our challenges because we are exposed to situations we may have never experienced. This fact holds true academically and professionally. Our experiences are not the same as others, nor are our outcomes, because we choose how we address challenges. A challenge can be the end of the world or an opportunity for advancement. As a mentor, I approach each situation with the mind-set of how we can move the ball forward.

The world needs you to make a difference. It has veered a long way from where it should be. You cannot always see the impact you are having on those around you. The little things you do may not make you famous, and they may seem to go unnoticed, but they can actually be a catalyst for something greater than you could ever imagine. Making a difference in this world sometimes means simply living every day as a creative light. By doing so, people may be changed by the authentic you. A million little actions can become a world-changing movement. No matter what we may think, everyone has a specific mission that can change the way we look at the world and the way people may look at us. Our ability to share our gifts stems from the challenges we receive through higher education. Even in experiencing those challenges, remember that the true sign of intelligence is not the knowledge you may receive but the imagination you will develop for what can be.

My strategy for achieving excellence in higher education was nothing more than *passion*. I called it continual forward progress. I had to have passion to finish what I started. There were times when I felt like giving up but the passion got me through. I also jumped at opportunities quicker than I jumped to conclusions as to what could or could not happen. Additionally, I quickly recognized that even when I did everything right, things could still go wrong. I used to think that doing the right things would protect me from bad situations, but that was just not true. Life introduces speed bumps, and that is all they should be – speed bumps. The only thing we can control in any given event is our reaction. Our preparation will have us walk while others may run. The way I ensured that I could walk was by making time to study. The only things that took priority over studying were church and family.

I smile a lot more. I used to be the hothead in the room, but I found that most people are not in the business of saying no simply to say no. I find myself searching for the way to yes more often than I argue a point. I have found that by listening more, I am able to articulate much better, which ultimately helps gain consensus on issues.

I have chosen to be part of the 3% of people who take things and change them on their own terms. Ninety-seven percent of people allow the world to dictate what happens and what they do. I also do all I can to remain humble, approachable, and credible. I read that words are singularly the most powerful force available to humanity. Therefore, I choose to use words of encouragement. Words have the energy and power to help, to heal, and to heat up the inner fire.

10
Quentin Newhouse, Jr., PhD, PCC, CPC

My dream of being a doctor started when I was about 5 years old, when some members of my family were involved in a serious car accident, although I was unharmed. While they were recovering in the hospital, I went on rounds and pretended to help the nurses serve their patients. I enjoyed the feeling of helping others.

I also remember playing doctor numerous other times when I was growing up. These play times were focused on probing, not actually helping people, assuming I could heal them. All of the boys learned quite quickly that the game was more fun when the patients were girls.

As far back as I can remember, my parents emphasized the importance of getting a college education. My parents told me that I could compete with anyone, regardless of their race and socioeconomic background. Both of my sisters, (one deceased) earned master's degrees in music and education. Although my father never completed a university degree, my mother achieved a PhD in guidance and counseling at the age of 66.

My father was a janitor, clothes presser, and cook (yes, he had three full-time jobs). He provided for us, but never had the opportunity to pursue his dreams to be a pharmacist. I remember him saying later in his life that everyone in our family had a degree except for him. I told him he had a PhD in my eyes (perfectly honorable dad). He smiled and agreed. I did not come from a family of financial privilege, where my success was ensured by my name or by a loan, gift, or large inheritance. My family sold all the property we jointly owned at the death of those persons who lived in those properties.

I want to believe that my experiences during my first semester of my freshman year at Marietta College (a small liberal arts college in rural Ohio) derailed my medical school aspirations. The combination of my first time away from home, taking Calculus as my first college math course, General Chemistry, General Biology, and other classes I can't recall made me lumber until my junior year with lower grades and lower expectations of being a doctor.

Although my first few years of college were disastrous from an academic perspective – I was even on academic probation – I remember saying to myself, "This school admitted me, so they were confident that I could do the work. I have to make it happen." I decided to pursue psychology for a major in my junior year of college. I loved the classes and achieved higher grades. In a testament to my scholarly ability, I even made the dean's list one semester.

When it was time to apply to graduate school, I prayed and realized that my overall C average, B+ average in psychology classes, and average scores on the graduate admissions tests were probably not going to land me in an Ivy League graduate psychology program or in any other graduate program. I applied to 10 schools and was rejected by all of them. My heart's intention was to attend Howard University, which is an HBCU close to my home in Washington, DC, and a program I believed graduated qualified psychologists.

When I was rejected from Howard University, I decided to write a letter to the chairperson in which I stated that they had made a mistake in not admitting me. To my surprise, I received a phone call inviting me to a meeting to discuss my candidacy. To my further surprise, the meeting consisted of being grilled by four professors on a panel for 2 hours on my psychology knowledge. After that forum was over, they all agreed that I had sufficient knowledge to pursue my graduate degree in psychology. I was provisionally admitted to see what I could do.

I had a stellar performance as a graduate student. My average was A-, and I secured a desirable graduate assistantship on a 4-year project that ended as my doctoral dissertation topic. While other students were scraping to find work, I was constantly employed and in the presence of my professors. I attribute prayer and hard work to my success as a graduate student.

I completed my master's degree in 3 years. By that time, my marriage to a fellow graduate student in psychology was crumbling, and I believe the stress on us was a major contributor to our divorcing shortly after I finished my master's. I then applied and was accepted to Howard's PhD program.

Due to numerous snafus and politics, it took me an additional 7 years to complete my doctorate; thus, I spent 10 years of my life working on two graduate degrees. Mind you, I did nothing but attend school and graduated at 30 as one of the youngest PhDs from the department at that time. Many years after I graduated, professors remembered how I fought to get in and to get out of graduate school. My doctoral dissertation defense lasted more than 2 hours and was attended by most of the faculty and many students. They all wanted to see this student whom they deemed a scrapper and to see if I had the goods to complete the program. By the grace of God I did and was as sane as one can be after that process.

Thirty-six students were admitted to the master's program when I started in 1971, but only four of us received our PhD. I had numerous mentors along the way to my doctorate. Some professors seemed to admire my tenacity and will to succeed. They gave me personal and professional advice, and I am forever indebted to their commitment to my success. I carried that commitment throughout my 40 years of academic and administrative experience as a professor, chair, and dean.

The five key attributes/characteristics that I possess are as follows:

- My strong faith in God and that I was created for a purpose other than just "sucking up air"
- My dogged determination that I can do whatever I set out to do, never give up, and find a way to achieve my objectives
- My will to consider alternative, innovative, and nontraditional ways to achieve my objectives
- My adaptive, keen wisdom and discernment about people and situations
- My desire to be a true servant and helper of those I serve

Another important point to make in my academic and professional accomplishments is that I am willing to accept constructive criticism from relevant others whenever it is necessary to achieve my goals. A sample of the long list of my on-the-way jobs includes dishwasher, waiter, telephone book deliverer, library assistant, and all-night cashier in a drugstore. I completed some of my degrees while working some of these jobs.

The same fortitude that it took for me to navigate graduate school has helped me to navigate my professional life. Both of my administrative experiences in academia were a result of being in the right place at the right time and stepping up to the plate. I volunteered to serve as an interim chair for five undergraduate and three graduate programs in a university because no one seemed to want the rotating chair position. As a result, I was a junior faculty member governing senior tenured faculty, many of whom had more than 20 years of experience over me. The department flourished under my leadership, including the design of the entire third floor of a new technology building and the establishment of the university's first Alcohol, Tobacco, and Other Drugs Prevention Center, which is still there after 20 years.

In the second experience, I wrote reports for the dean in a part-time, nontenured, nonbenefitted, hourly position. I was grateful to work as a psychologist in a business school. When the dean became ill, the president of the university offered me an interim position because he was aware I had the capability. I accepted and after 2 years in the position, the campus flourished in many ways, including the most improved among more than 60 other campuses.

Over more than 40 years of university and college teaching and administration, I estimated that I have taught more than 10,000 students. I hope that I inspired many of my former students who became college professors and administrators. I hear from them every now and then through venues such as LinkedIn and Facebook.

I have received many awards during my professional career, including several Who's Who in America, Black America, and Canada awards. My most cherished awards are the plaques, letters, cards, and gifts (including flasks, mugs, and pens) from my grateful students.

Although some professionals adhere to the specialist perspective, I have been blessed to pursue and master several career paths. I believe in diversity in professional experiences. I worked for the U.S. government, including 6 years as a computer specialist and social science statistician at the U.S. Census Bureau. I worked for Safeway, an international grocer, and as a director of an inner-city aftercare program with children ages 7–11.

I am an author and have published more than eight books and numerous chapters in books. I am particularly proud of two recent ongoing efforts. One of the projects involved editing a book with 25 men in Canada and the U.S. In the book, I asked them to share how they transitioned from adolescence to manhood. The resulting work is a testament of men aged 30 to 98 with varied strategies to manhood. The second project involved developing a series of children's books chronicling the lives of eight children who meet at a weekly tea party and find those events bond them throughout their lives.

After teaching and administering for more than 40 years, I decided to relocate to Canada after I married a Canadian. I left a great teaching job in North Carolina behind, sold my U.S. car to my wife for $1 to get it across the border, and have never regretted the decision to migrate north. In Canada, I have reinvented myself by taking coaching classes and achieving certification through the International Coaching Federation. I own the Canadian corporation Q

Newhouse Structured Coaching Strategies, Inc., and I have coached more than 80 clients over more than 2,500 paid hours.

I have dual U.S./Canadian citizenship and have been a member of the American Psychological Association, Eastern Psychological Association, Canadian Psychological Association, Society for Human Resource Management, and International Coaching Federation. I am also a member of the Montreal Board of Trade and Biz Montreal (a B2B group). Many of my coaching clients have come from my networking efforts.

If I can offer any words of wisdom or advice, they would be as follows:

- Have achievable goals and find reasonable ways to meet them
- Have several backup plans in case your primary plan fails
- Believe in your skill sets and master them so that they are marketable enough to provide for your everyday financial, emotional, and professional needs

- Network, network, network. Who you know can make a difference. There are people who do not have or need resumes simply because they are well connected.
- Getting reliable and consistent feedback about the quality and depth of your professional acumen is a crucial element of mastering one's craft.

My territory has been enlarged because I dared and still dare to dream beyond my personal or social circumstances. I determined and still do (I am 67 and not yet retired) that I am going to harness my desire to help others by making my rounds, helping where I can, probing people's desires, and assisting people toward their unrealized yet achievable dreams.

11
Dr. Terrance Knox

Childhood Influences

If we live long enough, we will face challenges in life, and I can say honestly that my life has been filled with them. Every person has a childhood background that is the basis of his or her dreams for the future. At an early age, I was highly motivated to become the best footballer, as well as a basketball player, but I was unsuccessful, although I invested all my effort in my dream. In my journey to achieve my childhood desire, I experienced a serious eye problem that did not simply postpone my dream, but prevented it from coming true. Thus, I suffered from low self-esteem as a child, because I too often fell short of reaching my goals.

Later, my interest shifted to being in the military. Many of my family members joined the military because it was a way to get out of the small town in South Carolina in which I was raised. My family members inspired me to pursue this goal, and I dedicated much of my time during high school to exercising because I had great expectations of becoming a military officer, just like many of my family members. I still remember it as if it was yesterday, making the 2.5-hour trip to Columbia for the physical examination required to enlist in the military. Having scored exceptionally well on the written part of the exam, I thought at the time that nothing would stop me from reaching my goal. However, because of my past problems with my eyes, I was rejected. At that time in my life, nothing seemed to be going my way, and I felt that I was a failure by comparison to others who had succeeded. I felt a great weight on my shoulders as I contemplated what I should do next, and many potential outcomes crossed my mind. My military recruiter encouraged me to write to my senator to have the decision overturned. Still feeling dejected, I decided to do so anyway and attempted to have the decision overturned. The process took months, and after exchanging letters back and forth with my senator, the original decision was upheld. Despite having fallen short of so many of my goals early in life, I still believed that I would have a breakthrough.

Educational Journey

After some thought, I decided to focus all of my attention on education, hoping that it would improve my life. At the time, I was not sure how far it could take me, but I knew I did not want to live my entire life in Pawley's Island, South Carolina. My journey to success required great determination and hard work because of the painful situations I had already experienced. At that time, I reflected on the past while embracing what lay ahead of me. I remembered something my second-grade teacher always told me, which was it is important that you do something that you enjoy in life. I had a passion for assembling things when I was a kid and was filled with boundless curiosity about complex puzzles. Therefore, I thought that I had an engineer in me, and without wasting another minute, I enrolled in an engineering course.

Although I was one of the best students in the class, I continued to be thwarted in my ambitions. Some of my problems were meant to strengthen my ability and test my patience. My great desire not to fail again was one of problems. I had to work hard to learn skills that would yield a satisfactory result, and my desire always woke me at dawn. Engineering was a field that required sacrifices to acquire the skills needed to be successful. Thus, I devoted much of my time to my studies and research to overcome my challenges. Thanks to hard work, persistence, and determination, I was able to get a job in a Fortune 500 organization and, after several years in the industry, I was promoted and became a project manager, which required stronger leadership skills. This was daunting, as I knew hardly anything about management.

This was not only a problem that required a solution, but it also challenged me to get out of my comfort zone. The post was a challenge because the engineering faculty focused on fixing problems and creating strong teams to develop solutions. I again struggled in my new environment. Luckily, I emerged victorious because hard work always has a reward. Because of my lack of knowledge in the area, I returned to school to obtain my MBA and a PhD.

Throughout my educational journey, my successes confirmed my academic acumen. I made many sacrifices and worked hard from the beginning. My mother, who also made great sacrifices for my brothers and me by working long hours – and sometimes working two or three jobs to provide for us – strongly motivated me. My three brothers had become successful in their military careers, and I invested and sacrificed much of my time to become who I wanted to be in life. My promotion to project manager was not only a challenge but also a tool that had positive effects on my life. The position influenced my professional career, as the more I worked, the more it challenged me to determine how I could help others achieve their potential. This stimulated my desire to teach and mentor others and became one of my passions as my interest in mentoring others grew.

Personal Attributes

Since an early age, five strong attributes have guided me and have contributed to me achieving my goals. Being a determined person was a major trait that helped me make wise decisions. Through determination, I was able to focus my efforts and energy on my goals. Many scholars define resolution as a coveted and laudable personality trait because it indicates one's motivation to be successful in life (Hamlin, 2006). Persistence was another attribute that contributed to my significant achievements, as it kept me moving forward, even after several disappointments, and enabled me to persist toward my later goals. I am also a disciplined person, which has helped me conquer life in all its aspects. The morals that my family inculcated in me provided a systematic way to approach all the challenges in my journey to higher education. Positive self-regard is a result of control as one achieves personal and professional success.

People can develop real virtues such as self-respect and self-confidence because of their morals, which increases their self-esteem. I acquired another attribute from my brothers, who were a positive influence in my life. I was also encouraged by African American men who experienced struggles similar to mine, which gave me a sense of brotherhood with those who had traveled the same path to obtain an education. Thus, I managed to share my ideas with those who could be considered successful and saw their high ideals as I interacted with them. Higher education equipped me with the skills that enabled me to obtain a job, and I gained valuable knowledge that supported my teaching career and ability to mentor others.

Open mindedness helps people strengthen their belief in themselves. A person can be honest and admit that no one is perfect and there is always room to improve. Finally, I have always been a good listener, which has enabled me to interact with people effectively. The skill to pay attention is one of the major attributes of a successful life. By paying attention, a person can develop more ideas that enhance his or her success. Higher education has had a positive influence on my ability to develop and grow professionally as well as personally. Because of what I gained, I was able to expand my skills and develop my ideas, and many areas of life into which I ventured improved. For example, I had to overcome my shyness about talking to people, which enabled me to be a mentor and to elevate and encourage others.

Obstacles in Obtaining My Higher Education Degree

Although I learned a lot through education, I encountered various obstacles along that path as well. However, I never gave up. One of the major obstacles I faced was the stiff competition I faced from more experienced scholars.

Therefore, I attended classes while teaching voluntarily at other learning institutions. I also developed my communication skills by joining Toastmasters and the John Maxwell Team.

As Neglia (2012) noted, membership forms the basis for achieving goals, as one can find support and share ideas. Being a member of various groups was another factor that contributed greatly to my success. These associations resulted from successful teamwork, which enabled me to seek more opportunities and expanded my expertise in professions with which I had been unfamiliar previously. I had the opportunity to join professional organizations I had never dreamt of joining before I became a member of them. The groups included the Supply Chain Organization, the John Maxwell Team, Project Management Institute, and Black Engineers National Society. Thus, I was able to learn and contribute more to the organizations, which had more experience and skills than I did.

Professional mentorship has played a large role in my ability to cross the hills and valleys of life in pursuit of success. People who develop a good mentoring relationship can meet their personal and career development needs

(Carter, 2003). Mentorship provides techniques and tips that set individuals on the path to achieve their goals in life. By participating in such programs, a person can establish a productive career. Following others' footsteps enabled me to develop confidence and competence.

I greatly appreciate mentorship as a part of my professional growth. By sharing my knowledge and skills in the many organizations I joined, I was able to respond to the programs in a positive way by mentoring others who wished to grow both professionally and personally. I was also able to acquire and enhance coaching and interpersonal skills, both of which were factors in my success.

I participate in mentorship to help as many people as possible, because other successful individuals voluntarily inspired me to become who I am. Mentorship has provided me with an opportunity to build critical interpersonal skills, which I want to give back to society. It is also my responsibility to ensure my mentees evaluate different alternatives to achieve their goals, as the third choice I made surpassed all my previous ones. I have taught them how to develop actions and plans based on their mentor's responses or feedback, just as I used to do. Because of the excellent lessons I received from a willing mentor, I feel the responsibility to help as many people as possible.

Although I have experienced many challenges along the way, I can now enjoy the fruits of my determination, hard work, and persistence. This has given me a great desire to share some words of wisdom with many young people whose ambitions are similar to mine. First, I urge all of them to be determined to seek and fulfill their dreams. They ought to remain focused and determined, as becoming successful is a process. I also suggest that they emulate some of my attributes, including discipline, determination, open-mindedness, persistence, and good listening skills, as they all contribute to my ultimate success. Finally, I urge them to put more effort into their endeavors and be ready to give back to society. Young people have energy and the ability to make the best out of situations. They are also in a position to make wise decisions in life through mentorship. If young people put these recommendations into practice, they can achieve success in life.

I used certain approaches to excel in higher education. I learned the importance of remaining humble and hungry, which enabled me to persevere in all aspects of life.

Humility and self-denial were among the major factors that contributed to my ability to achieve my objectives. I also realized the importance of helping others on their own journeys to success, which will uplift them and perhaps benefit all of society. I also recognized the need for commitment and sacrifice in everything I did, because I could not be successful without them. I also considered personal growth a process through which people must go before they can reach their potential in life. The approaches I used assisted me greatly in accomplishing my goals, because had I not adopted the strategies, I believe my efforts would have been in vain.

My education has been an example for others. I decided not to hide my school achievements, because by becoming educated, the younger generation can have an influence on the entire nation. Therefore, I use my educational background and join others who have succeeded in life to steer development in the country. I am also looking forward to using my mentorship experience to contribute to raising a nation of successful young people who can make significant contributions to their countries. Moreover, I am creating awareness about how to be successful in life among as many people as I can.

Challenges shape a person's character and life. One can either yield to difficult circumstances or overcome them. I believe there are no coincidences, everything happens for a reason, and our reactions to life events determine the path we will follow. Challenges in my life led me to personal and professional growth I could not have imagined. For instance, I never dreamed that one day I would be able to change people's lives for the better by becoming a mentor and role model, but I did. Because of my shyness, I could not imagine being able to speak in front of an audience and share my knowledge and experience, both in my country and abroad. I could also not imagine becoming a project manager because it entailed managing people and projects, which was my weakest set of skills at one time. All the positive changes in my life were a result of hard work, determination, persistence, and sacrifices. My journey to higher education has not only increased my knowledge, but also become a great tool in mentoring and coaching young people all over the world. Now, I believe it is my turn to inspire and guide people to become who they want to be.

References

Carter, C. B. (2003). *Keys to success in college, career, and life: How to achieve your goals.* Upper Saddle River, NJ: Prentice Hall.

Hamlin, S. (2006). *How to talk so people listen: Connecting in today's workplace*. New York, NY: Collins.

Neglia, J. (2012). *Onward and upward*. Bloomington, IL: Author House.

12
Otis Johnson, PhD, MPA

A person who never made a mistake never tried anything new.

—Albert Einstein

Growing Up

My life began in a rural part of Jamaica, where very few people had a chance to go to high school and almost no one went to college. I am part of a huge family and was constantly competing for attention from my parents and older brothers and sisters. One day, an aunt persuaded my mother to send me to middle school in a nearby town, where I would have a chance of proceeding on to high school. After raising several objections, including the fact that she thought I would get hit by a car because I did not know how to cross the street in a city with cars around, my mother finally agreed.

Growing up in a small remote village limits one's expectations of possibilities to some extent. This was certainly true for me in a small community where no one had a car until I was about 9 years old. The first time I saw a car, I thought it was a futuristic machine being driven by some kind of superhero I heard about in stories from my neighbor who had relatives in England. I was so fascinated by that moment that I knew right then I wanted to be a driver when I grew up. Throughout my youth, my perception of the ideal profession changed multiple times, mainly due to new experiences and interactions. My career aspirations shifted from driver to superhero to lawyer to doctor to president. In other words, I had no idea what I wanted to do when I grew up.

Middle school went by quickly, and I passed the high school entrance exam for one of the most prestigious boarding schools in the country. From there, I went on to the University of Technology, where I got an honors diploma in medical technology and was elected the science department representative in the student government. In my role as the representative, I founded and ran an educational game show similar to Jeopardy. Students in the various science programs competed against each other, and the game became a major weekly attraction for the entire department. I won the award for most outstanding department representative that year and was nominated for the university's Student of the Year Award.

Migration to the United States

Upon my arrival in the United States, I found it difficult to get a job as a medical technologist because I had foreign educational credentials and had only done a 6-week internship at Cornwall Regional Hospital. Consequently, I ended up doing odd jobs to pay the bills. These jobs included package delivery, book sales, and telemarketing. These were challenging for me, as I had never done anything similar before and found them difficult and stressful. I even contemplated returning to Jamaica, where my job was a lot easier and I got more respect. However, a friend and former classmate had migrated to New York a few years earlier and encouraged me to hang in there.

Once I was settled, I started attending Hunter College of the City University of New York, where I ended up redoing several of the courses I had already taken in Jamaica. Of course I found this frustrating, but was determined to get a degree in the United States so that I could simply get a decent job. I reflected on my wild, childhood dreams of becoming a doctor and of becoming president. At that point in my life, I found myself simply aiming for a good job. This was quite ironic, but I felt the need to lower my expectations so that I would not be disappointed any further by the pressures associated with assimilating into my new environment. Based on the negative experiences I had finding a job, I felt it was dangerous to have high aspirations because the consequences of not achieving them could be even more devastating.

Major Dilemma

I had interesting experiences in Economics and English Literature, two of the first classes I took at Hunter College. Having struggled for 2 years to save enough money to pay for the courses, I was determined to learn everything I could and to do well in them. In Economics, I completed every single exercise in the study guide twice and was the only student who earned an A+. The professor implored me to change my major and promised prestigious internships on Wall Street. The experience was a little different in the English Literature class, but was along the same lines. My first assignment was to critique the play *Antigone*. In doing so, I immersed myself into the play and compared Antigone and Creon's experiences to my childhood desires to own a bicycle. I was promised one, but never received it. As a result, I always tempered my expectations because I was afraid of what I perceived as a major letdown. To my surprise, the professor read my paper in front of the class and described it as her idea of excellence. For the second time, I declined to change my major and stuck with science.

After completing my honors degree at Hunter College, I conducted HIV research in an immunology laboratory at New York University (NYU) School of Medicine before moving on to become a clinical research scientist at Merck & Co., Inc., one of the world's largest pharmaceutical companies. At NYU School of Medicine, I worked as a laboratory technician processing samples and running various assays in the immunology research laboratory.

Transition to the Pharmaceutical Industry

In May 2000, I made a career move from basic research to clinical research at Merck, because I felt that this would give me an opportunity to use more of my people skills. My first 6 years at Merck were spent researching and developing medicines for respiratory conditions such as asthma, exercise-induced bronchospasm, allergy, and chronic obstructive pulmonary disease. My work involved researching, consulting with respiratory experts, and working with physicians to design and conduct clinical research studies. I also had the opportunity to coauthor several protocols and clinical study reports that became part of drug applications submitted to the Food and Drug Administration and other regulatory agencies worldwide. Prior to the launch of a clinical trial, we conducted investigator meetings to orient the participating physicians, nurses, and study coordinators to the protocol. I presented the protocol procedures and conducted spirometry training sessions at these worldwide meetings.

I coauthored three abstracts related to my work in the respiratory therapeutic area at Merck. One of my abstracts and poster presentation was selected for publication in the *Journal of Allergy and Clinical Immunology*. It was also noted among the most interesting presentations at the 2003 American Academy of Asthma, Allergy and Immunology annual meeting in San Antonio, Texas.

My transition from the scientific side of the business to operations was not easy, as I feared I was destroying great relationships with the head of the respiratory and immunology department and my manager. They both wanted to retain me in the group because of my strong performance record and the expertise I developed in spirometry training, data collection, and analysis. However, I was aware that moving up in a scientific role at the time for non-physician staff was more the exception than the rule. At the same time, I noticed that it was becoming increasingly difficult to find patients interested in participating in clinical trials. I also learned of a small group of people in Merck's clinical operations group who were studying patient enrollment problems and became fascinated with some of the initial ideas they had.

I always had a keen eye for identifying ways to improve efficiency and frequently did value-added work outside my core job description. One notable value-added project I did as a clinical scientist was writing and producing a professional-grade training video to reduce costs associated with worldwide travel to train trial nurses, physicians, and study coordinators how to perform quality lung-function tests consistently.

Because of this project, I was asked to participate in a major restructuring initiative at Merck to improve the efficiency of its scientific and operational divisions. This project led to the creation of a dedicated patient recruitment and feasibility department intended to create discipline and focus on processes to facilitate better planning and execution of clinical trials. The initial focus of the department was on better country and site selection, as well as improved predictability through patient recruitment planning. I later joined this dedicated group and founded a clinical informatics function that provided the analytics that supported feasibility and patient recruitment for clinical trials. My team and I began tracking metrics rigorously and were able to show that when we were involved in planning and running clinical trials, the trials were more likely to finish on time. These performance metrics were largely responsible for the team making it through the Merck-Schering Plough merger fully intact, while there were large employee reductions in other parts of the company.

Turning Point

On one occasion, my manager asked me and the other managers in the group to prepare a plan documenting how each of our groups would add value that year. He later approached me with the three plans and asked if I could help him figure out which components of the plans would make the most sense for the group as a whole. I used a modified version of the decision tree model with revenue projection to show how elements of the three plans could contribute to improved clinical trial implementation. This was a tool I learned about in one of my management classes. "Now I know why we are funding your PhD" was his comment at the end of the exercise. This was just one of several ways I applied new knowledge from the courses I was enrolled in, which is one of the values of working full time while going to school. It also gave me great case studies to use in class discussions and assignments. I sought every opportunity to use the new knowledge I was acquiring to transform the way I handled decision challenges on the job. My manager then saw me as a more useful strategic resource.

This interaction was a key turning point in my career, as it led to my ultimate introduction to Ramita Tandon, the most influential figure to date in my career development. I met Ramita through pure chance. I was on a business trip when I received a phone call from a former boss. He appeared to be in a hurry, worried, desperate, and was speaking very fast. Despite those challenges, I learned that one of his speaking partners dropped out at the last minute and he needed someone to join a panel the next day to discuss the use of electronic health records in clinical research. I had worked on a few relevant projects, so I adjusted my travel plans to join the speaker panel. Ramita was one of the speakers.

A year later, I received a phone call from Ramita. She informed me of a job opportunity to fix a problem in a feasibility group at a contract research organization (CRO). I was a little skeptical about leaving a top-tier pharmaceutical company to work for a CRO, but was curious about the issues that needed remediation. Chief among the issues was a perception that the group was not data driven and was not really much of a feasibility group. Having solved a similar problem at Merck, I felt confident and decided to explore the opportunity. During the interview, Ramita showed me the organization chart she wanted to proceed with once I joined. There was one position reporting into her, the senior vice president and general manager, and another senior position reporting into the head of the feasibility group. She circled the position reporting into her and said, "That is where I want to place you." I struggled, but managed, to hide my excitement. Finally, someone recognized my capabilities and was willing to give me a senior-enough position matching my true capabilities.

I joined the CRO to lead the group and prove to Ramita that she made the right decision. I rapidly transformed the existing feasibility group into a state-of-the-art feasibility and clinical informatics function, a result I won an operational excellence award for and a promotion to vice president. I did this by making better use of the existing data assets the company had access to, introducing new data sources and decision-making tools, and hiring dedicated clinical informatics professionals to crunch data and make better sense of them. A large part of my success in this role was a result of the strong support and mentoring Ramita provided. During my first month, a senior vice president of project management challenged my work, citing her experience as the reason for the challenge with no other data to support her position. Ramita stepped in, cited my data-driven analysis, and reminded the team of my strong academic and professional background. I gained a lot of respect and became quite influential in the organization from that point on. Ramita continues to be a mentor, advocate, and friend.

I hold a health science undergraduate degree from Hunter College of the City University of New York, a master of public administration in health policy and management from New York University (NYU), and a PhD in management from Walden University. During my undergraduate study, I did extensive theory and laboratory coursework in immunology, biochemistry, biotechnology, pathology, anatomy, and physiology. Such coursework gave me a sound scientific foundation for my career, but it lacked the balance I needed for a scientific leadership career, which led me to pursue the master of public administration in health policy and management, where I learned health statistics, health economics, health policy, process improvement, and human resources management. My focus then shifted to developing decision-making skills and expertise in modeling, simulation, and clinical trial enrollment forecasting, skills that would be needed for more senior leadership roles. The PhD in management with a specialization in leadership and organizational change was a key tool to build the competencies I sought.

Since I stumbled upon clinical research accidentally while separating cells in the lab at NYU School of Medicine, my professional goal has been to become a senior executive in the pharmaceutical industry. I have also maintained an interest in management consulting and have done a few consulting projects. To achieve these goals, I felt it necessary to balance my on-the-job experience with formal education at the doctoral level so that people would take me seriously.

As vice president of a fairly large company in the pharmaceutical industry with oversight responsibility for more than 100 people, I am living that dream. I am regularly invited to speak in front of large audiences, including the annual Drug Information Agency meeting, which attracts thousands each year. The Drug Information Agency is one of a few carefully selected professional organizations of which I am a member. Membership in these professional organizations gives me access to other professionals working on innovations of interest and a network to seek answers to questions and to hear other perspectives.

Mentoring and Giving Back

I have had very good mentoring relationships throughout my academic and professional career. At one point during the PhD program, my dissertation chair and mentor left the program, leaving me worried, as students usually take longer to complete the program when they lose their chair. An existing committee member, Dr. Branford McAllister, took over as my chair and suggested that I ask Dr. Walter McCollum to join my dissertation committee as a mentor. Dr. McCollum said yes and exceeded my expectations. Every time I submitted my dissertation or components of it for review, Dr. McCollum reviewed my work and provided written feedback within 24–48 hours, even though the university requirement was set at 14 days. Dr. McAllister was also very effective, as he provided specific direction and feedback that were easy to act on. These two outstanding professors accelerated my academic achievements and effectively helped me move onward and upward.

Serving as a mentor and giving back has always been important to me. I regularly provide academic and career advice to high school and college students. I have also provided financial assistance by paying tuition and buying books and uniforms for a set of students in a nursing program, as well as a program for adults who wanted to learn to read. I have provided capital and business advice to several relatives and friends to support their start-ups. These businesses include four small chicken farms in the village I grew up, a day-care facility, a commercial fishing company, a retail store, a restaurant, and three health-care-industry consulting businesses.

The value of these mentoring relationships, together with my academic and professional experiences, lies in the key success factors I was able to isolate. I have highlighted some of the most important of these factors here to help others move onward and upward.

Keys to Success

One of the keys to success is to identify the attributes and specific skills needed to succeed in your current role and the one you desire. This could be a skill you acquire as a result of taking on and solving a pressing problem in your department. You then become the go-to person when a similar need arises and a valuable asset to your organization in the process.

Learn what is expected of you in your role from the start. If specific, measurable goals are not set for you, create them yourself and discuss them with your manager. Doing so will help you focus. I have come across many situations in which I was asked to take on substantial projects not aligned with any of my established performance goals. The response I was usually given when I asked for clarification and the connection with my goals was that we need to do whatever is needed for the business. Doing what is needed for the business is absolutely right and you should absolutely do it, but adjust your performance goals to include those projects. Those projects should now be your focus. Your time is a limited resource, and although you can attempt to do everything, you will not be able to do all of them really well.

Do not get fixated on perfection. It is expensive and time consuming. It is often more important to get the project done and improve from there. This is an area I have spent time developing over the years, as I often found myself spending too much time trying to make things perfect. As a result, I tended to feel I never had enough time to get everything accomplished. Finding that balance between perceived perfection and getting tasks accomplished is my idea of excellence, but I consciously guard against the waste associated with seeking perfection.

Learn various research methods, problem-solving, and decision-making skills. They will be valuable in work and personal situations. While your end goal may be to earn a degree, obtain your dream job, or receive a promotion, you need to master the methods, so you can apply them in new situations and different environments. A former boss, who is also a college professor, once told me that it does not matter what I get my PhD in. What matters, he said, is an understanding of the process of scientific inquiry, development of a sound research methodology, strong writing skills, and the ability to express ideas clearly. I think he is right because these competences will certainly help you move onward and upward.

13
Jonas Nguh, PhD, RN

Professor

Education is the most powerful weapon that we can use to change the world.
— Nelson Mandela

What were your childhood influences that sparked your connection to higher education?

I was born and raised in a family that valued education, and my parents worked hard to provide the best quality education. From a very young age, the importance of education was instilled in me, not only as a means of ending poverty but also because an education would prepare me to take advantage of the many wonderful opportunities that world has to offer. As the last of seven children, all my siblings were educated to a postsecondary level, and it went without saying that I too would follow in those steps. I grew up in an environment where resources where limited, and I knew that the only way I would accomplish my goals would be to get an education. As I advanced my education to the postsecondary level, I began to realize the benefits of graduate and postgraduate education, and I knew that if I wanted to function at the level at which I intended, then I needed an advanced degree and professional credentials. Identifying where I wanted to be (having a goal in mind) was the impetus that spurred me on and directed not only my choice of career but also the jobs and roles within which I now function.

Describe your educational journey? What were the challenges you were faced by and how did you overcome them? What were the successes that confirmed your academic acumen, scholarship and educational journey?

I began my education journey from the diploma level, where I obtained a certificate in nursing as a caregiver (certified nurse's aide) and moved along the career advancement path to a licensed practical nurse, to a registered nurse, to a baccalaureate degree in nursing, to two graduate degrees (nursing and healthcare administration), and a doctorate in public health. The most significant challenge to me was finances. Higher education is an expensive endeavor to undertake, and my underprivileged background and circumstances meant that resources were limited and the cost of education had to be considered. Most of my education had to be funded personally, and this meant a longer than expected education journey, as I had to work to obtain the funds to pay for the classes. Another challenge was not knowing how to navigate the educational system or knowing what resources, organizations, and support were available. This severely impacted my success in the sense that for most of my academic journey, I had to take the long route for most things or only found out after the fact that it could have been done it differently or that resources or support were available. As I progressed along my trajectory, each academic accomplishment served as a motivation for me to attain the next level. These successes were the primary factor that kept me going, as I knew that the sacrifices being made were worth it and I was achieving my goals.

How did your educational career influence your professional career?

I was born and raised in an environment afflicted with many health disparities, such as limited access to care, limited financing to pay for care, a shortage of healthcare providers and physicians, high rates of health illiteracy, and marginalization of vulnerable groups. From a young age, I knew I wanted to address these issues. This desire led me to my profession in public health. Although I did not know how this desire to affect change would be translated into a professional career, as I grew up and advanced in my educational journey, it became much clearer to me where my passion lay and how I could align my passion with a career. I began my professional career as a registered nurse based on the desire to make an impact in my community. Nursing provided me the opportunity to impact lives on an individual basis as a bedside nurse. I knew that I wanted to affect change on a much larger scale and a broader level, so I continued my education at an advanced level and obtained a master's of science in nursing and a master's of science in healthcare administration. I also earned a PhD in public health specializing in disease prevention and education. My education provided the perfect triangulation for my career, as I am competent in all three arms of health services delivery (clinical, administrative, and global), and it allows me to function in any or all of the above roles. Most of my work is focused on developing and strengthening health systems in low-resource countries. This work is informed greatly by my education, in the sense that I focused my interest on vulnerable and marginalized communities and populations to develop and enhance health care systems and reduce many of the healthcare disparities I witnessed so often as a child.

What are five key attributes/characteristics that you possess as the cornerstone of your achievement?

Key attributes that I possess as a cornerstone of my achievement include a desire for lifelong learning, being self-reflective, staying open to new opportunities, taking risks and not being afraid of failure, and learning from failure. One of the keys to success is knowing that learning is a lifelong process and that people continue to grow and develop. This is an area that I continue to illustrate in my career. Lifelong learning provides me with the knowledge and tools to remain current and relevant in my practice and the credibility required to affect change. Being self-reflective is an important element that ensures I am able to identify areas of weakness and growth, as I can then tailor my strategy to address those areas. Taking calculated risks, not being afraid of failure, and learning from mistakes are equally important elements. Any successful individual will tell you that those elements carry a lot of weight in determining their success. My desire for success has always been, and continues to be, greater than my fear of failure. And when failure occurs, as it inevitably will, I will learn from the situation and will not repeat the same mistakes.

How has earning a higher education influenced your ability to grow and develop personally and professionally?

Higher education has opened the door to a new world of opportunities and possibilities for me. It has given me the professional credibility and visibility needed to affect change at a broader level. It has provided me the opportunity to serve on professional organizations and leadership committees, to be a guest or visiting lecturer at several institutions of higher learning, and to conduct and participate in research projects and speak in front of peers at several international conferences. Additionally, higher education has enhanced my proficiency to prepare and apply for research grants and use the funding received in several social change projects that address health disparities and income inequalities, alleviate poverty, and provide safe living conditions in vulnerable communities around the world.

What were some of the obstacles you've had to face post earning a higher degree? How were you able to overcome the obstacles?

Although earning a higher education degree presents many advantages and opportunities, it would be unfair to claim that no obstacles remain. For the most part, the challenges are the same before and after earning a higher degree. The difference at this level is that our awareness increases, and we are better prepared to identify and navigate those obstacles. Unique to the African American male perspective, which is similar to my own experience, are some of the obstacles faced, which include a lack of representation of African American males in leadership roles, both in academic and practice settings; a dearth of resources and support designed specifically for African American men; limited opportunities for advancement; and lack of diversity (gender, cultural, racial, generational) initiatives in institutions. These obstacles present a ceiling for the advancement of African American men in work settings and limit the potential of many well-qualified and talented individuals.

How important has membership in professional organizations contributed to your academic achievement? Which professional organizations are you a member of?

My professional career is based primarily in the field of nursing and public health, and membership in professional organizations is expected in this field, as these are service-based professions. I am a member of several professional organizations, including the American Public Health Association, American Nurses Association, National League of Nursing, American Association for Men in Nursing, American College of Healthcare Executives, and National Academy of Practice. The importance of membership in professional organizations cannot be overemphasized. Membership is expected in certain career fields and demonstrates commitment and dedication or service to the profession through the paying of dues, journal subscriptions, advocacy for certain causes, and commitment to lifelong learning. Benefits of membership in professional organizations include networking opportunities with other members, career resources and job opportunities, continuing education credits, professional certifications, and credentials that illustrate competency in one's area of interest. As is the case with many health-related professions, membership in professional associations enhances academic and career progression through earning relevant credentials. Many of the resources, learning materials, tools, and short courses provided to members enable them to gain particular knowledge, leadership competencies, and skills required to function at many senior and executive levels.

How important has professional mentorship been in your ability to move onward and upward, both academically and professionally?

African American men often have limited access to and opportunities for professional mentorship. This was certainly the case with my own experience as I moved up the career ladder. Being in a predominantly female profession (nursing), there were almost no role models for male nurses in general and specifically African American male nurses that I could look up to and model myself after. Thus, I often learned lessons through trial and error, and only after making mistakes would I know what to do (or not to do) the next time. After obtaining my doctorate, I actively pursued having a formal mentorship and began benefitting from the value of that relationship. Even though I am in the mid phase of my career, I have been able to benefit, and continue to benefit, from this relationship in moving my career toward a more strategic path and aligning myself with my passion and professional goals.

What is your association with mentorship? How have you mentored others to move onward and upward?

Mentorship is one of the areas that I have a particular love for and am most concerned about. In 2015, I was honored to be awarded the Outstanding Mentor award from the Maryland Nurses Association. This award is given to an individual who best demonstrates outstanding efforts and interest in the professional development and advancement of less experienced nurses. I believe that our success is determined by the role models in our lives, and this is certainly true in my own situation. I have already benefited, and continue to benefit, from the many mentors that I have in my professional life whose wise counsel and wealth of experience I have used in times of doubt or uncertainly or as a model for my career trajectory. Mentorship is particularly important for African American males given their underrepresentation in many senior or executive leadership roles and positions. I have launched and implemented several mentorship initiatives, such as the Minority Men Initiative at a local community college, that prepare African American males for success during their tenure at the institution and deal with issues often taken for granted, such as preparing for job interviews, writing resumes, developing work habits, coping with work conflict, and developing communication styles. In my view, mentorship is not about preparing a person for a job, but rather providing the requisite skills and knowledge so that person can take advantage of opportunities that arise.

What are some words of wisdom you would like to share with young men who are aspiring higher personally and professionally?

With 20 years of career experience, there is a wealth of wisdom that I could share, but I will limit it to just a few suggestions. The first suggestion is to understand the importance of being resilient. Resilience refers to the ability or capacity to recover from difficulties. Anyone who has been in a leadership role or position will encounter challenges sooner or later. Resilience is how we pick ourselves back up and move forward. Quitting is not an option. Remember, "Tough times never last, but tough people do." A second suggestion for words of wisdom is to "build your roof before it rains." We often learn our lessons the hard way, which is after the problem has occurred. I had to learn this lesson myself after making mistakes because I was not proactive in my approach toward issues.

At this point in my career, I understand and articulate the importance of being proactive with concerns or situations that require my attention so that molehills do not become mountains and less time is spent putting out fires that did not have to exist in the first place. The third suggestion is to have a growth plan. People often seem to go with the flow and do not have a specific trajectory for their career or path. However, the most successful individuals in their personal and professional lives are those who have identified a clearly defined path and then aligned their actions along that chosen path. Success is not accidental, and we need to be strategic regarding what we do and how we do it to bring about success. Another suggestion is to understand the importance of seeing adversity the right way. No matter who we are and where we are, we are likely to encounter disappointments, rejection, or adversity. After we have cried over the spilled milk, we need to move on and use the incident as a learning opportunity from which to grow and develop. I have made lots of mistakes in my career, but it is in those hard times when I thought all was lost that I have grown the most. I realize now that we are challenged in the difficult times, and that is where our best growth opportunities occur. Other words of wisdom include "be a people builder," as our success depends on the people around us and how much they do or do not support us; "turn off the negative voices" because negative voices will keep you from your path and prevent you from fulfilling your purpose; and finally "recognize which battles to fight." One of the most important lessons I have learned in life is that if you are going somewhere, you cannot stop to throw stones along the way.

What was your step-by-step strategy/approach to achieving excellence in higher education (tools, systems, processes, tips)?

One strategy that I used as I pursued my graduate education was reaching out to friends or colleagues who had completed the same degree program. This strategy helped me understand what to expect and how to plan and prepare for any challenges that I might encounter during the course of my studies. A second strategy I used was prioritization. One of the most commonly cited reasons for failing to complete higher education is that people have unrealistic expectations regarding the amount of time, energy, and dedication required at this level, given the rigor, intensity, quality, and content of materials expected. Pursuing higher education means that something has to give. I had to cut back on social functions and personal and leisure activities so that I could dedicate that time to my studies. The strategy of time management is equally as important. Given that the typical higher education student is an adult learner who has a full-time job and a family, effective time management is crucial for success. I had to plan out and set aside specific days and times for completing assignments, reading course materials, and participating in the required activities. This was probably the most effective contributing factor to my success, as I had to strike a balance between family, work, and studies and still be successful without negatively affecting any of these areas.

What were some key lessons learned about yourself that demonstrates personal growth?

One of the most important lessons I learned about myself is that my motivation for success is far greater than my fear of failure. This may be one of the most important lessons for anyone who desires to advance in whatever they do. I realized that despite the challenges and limitations I faced, my desire to be successful outweighed any fears that I had. Another lesson I learned is that I had the skills, knowledge, and abilities needed to be successful. Self-doubt about our own abilities and competencies may prevent us from taking the next step or moving forward, but when we take the first step, we realize that this is something we can do.

How are you using your educational achievement to change the world? How has your territory been enlarged?

I am a leader in the area of maternal and infant health. Over the past 20 years, I have made significant and sustained contributions in maternal and infant health care across three continents. In Sub-Saharan Africa, approximately 830 women die daily from preventable causes related to pregnancy and childbirth. Women in Africa have a 1 in 16 chance of dying in pregnancy or childbirth, compared to a 1 in 4,000 chance in a developed country. This disparity led me to create an entrepreneurial model for maternity homes based on microeconomy principles and established as a community cooperative in which local stakeholders are responsible for its management and governance. This model takes the form of a residential obstetric facility where women can await their delivery and have antenatal care services and medical and nursing staff available. The fact that this model has been successfully replicated and is currently implemented in four countries (India, Senegal, Uganda, and Zambia) demonstrates its potential to impact future generations. Two million women have accessed services from these maternity homes, and expanding the program to three more countries has the potential to reach 5 million additional women. I have founded several community service organizations, including United Vision for Women, Sari Women Initiative, and Sickle Cell Aid Foundation. Staff members of the United Vision for Women organization in East Africa work to improve the lives of young women at risk for early and forced marriages through theater and the arts to engage communities and change attitudes to achieve better sexual and reproductive health for teenage girls. Membership has increased to more than 1,000 teenage girls in five schools. The Sari Women Initiative works to provide support and education for women in rural Kenya to address intimate partner violence, forced marriages, and female genital mutilation. The initiative has created three women-owned businesses that produce affordable menstrual pads for girls and women. Staff members of the Sickle Cell Aid Foundation in West Africa work to educate and inform young people about their condition and encourage them to get tested to know their hemoglobin genotype. This organization has expanded to four African countries.

14
Walter R. McCollum, PhD

Dean of Student Affairs, Walden University

President, McCollum Enterprises, LLC

Executive Director, Walter McCollum Education Foundation

Every great dream begins with a dreamer. Always remember, you have within you the strength, the patience, and the passion to reach for the stars to change the world.
—Harriet Tubman

Dreaming is something that I have always done! While growing up in a small town in South Carolina, I remember dreaming of a better life, dreaming of opportunities to travel the world and earn an education, and dreaming of using my life to change the world in some way. Dreams were all that I had to hold onto in the midst of the plights and social conditions that surrounded me. I grew up as an only child in the 60s and 70s in a single-parent household where my mother worked two jobs to provide for me. My father did what he could to provide for me, but with another family of his own, he was stretched thin. I had a village of family members who stood in the gap for both my mother and father because of the love they had for us as family. My parents only lived 9 miles apart, so it was relatively easy for both sides of the family to come together to provide love and support. Both sides of the family are like one big family, and my mother and father have always been friends. I can literally say, "It takes a village to raise a child."

I was fortunate and remain grateful that I was reared by, and had the opportunity to know, both sets of great-grandparents. Many wonderful experiences and lessons contributed to the man I have become. My maternal great-grandparents owned a farm that included almost every farm animal imaginable. I would follow Grandpa to milk the cows, plow the fields, cut pulpwood, bale hay, feed the chickens and hogs, and so much more. I would watch Grandma churn butter and buttermilk, gather eggs from the nests, and pick many fruit and vegetables – peas, beans, potatoes, tomatoes, corn, okra, peanuts, strawberries, and blackberries. Boy, those homemade blackberry and strawberry pies were delicious! The work ethic was strong on both sides of the family. I am thankful to my late great-grandparents for instilling a good work ethic in me at a very young age. My paternal great-grandparents and grandparents were my rock and foundation. They kept me in church and grounded in the word of God. They were very empathetic and supportive, understood the plights and social conditions that I faced, and always encouraged me to continue fighting and pushing through. My grandfather stood in the gap for my father and talked with me about life, education, and changing the world. I remember Papa retiring from Draper Corporation after working there for over 40 years, serving the elderly in his community, serving as an honorary deacon in his church, serving as Santa for the children in the community, and giving his last dime to help someone. He was a family man, modest and humble, with a quiet spirit. I always dreamed of being like him. Little did I know that my dream would come true, and I would continue his legacy.

When I was 7 years old, I awoke from a dream in which I was walking across a stage in a cap and gown to receive a diploma. I heard the name "Dr. Walter McCollum," but in the dream I was a child walking across the stage to receive my diploma. Unbeknownst to me, God was showing me a glimpse of the beginning of a profound life that would lead to positive social change. I shared the dream with Papa, and he encouraged me to earn the highest level of education possible and to be an example for others in the community to follow. That is what I did. After graduating from high school, I entered the U.S. Air Force at the age of 17. Because I was not old enough to enlist, my father signed for me. That was the best decision I could have made to change the trajectory of my life from growing up in a small town where there were high rates of domestic abuse, drug and alcohol abuse, broken families, and sexual abuse. I have lost relatives to cirrhosis of the liver due to drinking alcohol every day. I lived through the trauma of seeing my mother and other women beaten by men. These experiences, compounded with friends of the family attempting to molest me, led to a state of manic depression and to suicide attempts. This was during an era when many parents provided for their children but were not equipped to nurture, guide, and provide practical support to them. Pathological behavior is passed down from generation to generation until someone decides to break the cycle and break the curse. I broke the cycle and broke the curse. It was not until I broke the cycle of pathological behavior that I was able to connect with my purpose and passion. Our lives are often consumed with so much stuff, baggage, and brokenness that we are not able to see the forest for the trees. We are often so busy that we do not have the quietness or solitude needed to align to our faith, which is a key ingredient to aligning with purpose and passion.

I have often heard that purpose and passion are birthed from pain. I believe this is true, as the years of pain that I lived through definitely led me to my purpose. During my years in the Air Force, I enrolled in college, joined various ministries in church, and volunteered in communities where I was stationed. Despite the aftermath from the plights I had experienced, I was still holding onto my dreams and trying to apply the foundational principles that I learned growing up. I also went through years of counseling to overcome the trauma and depression I was experiencing. I am grateful that I did not fall prey to the idea that going to counseling is a sign of weakness and a stigma. Little did I know that I would write a book for men titled *Strength of a Black Man: Destined for Self-Empowerment* to encourage Black men to go to counseling to overcome thoughts of suicide or other plights they faced, such as absentee fathers, lack of supportive and positive role models and mentors, physical abuse, domestic abuse, and even sexual abuse.

I traveled the world while serving in the Air Force. Over my 13-year service obligation, I was stationed at Langley

Air Force Base in Hampton, Virginia; Clark Air Base in the Philippines; Ellsworth Air Force Base in Rapid City, South Dakota; Incirlik Air Base in Turkey; Virginia Military Institute in Lexington, Virginia; and Bolling Air Force Base and the Pentagon in Washington, DC. In the Philippines, I started to connect with my purpose and passion of serving in other countries. I was only 19 and felt a need to engage in the betterment of humankind. Right outside the military base, small children were living in cardboard boxes. Some had no clothes and looked like they had not eaten in months. Through the base chapel, I helped men in the men's ministry volunteer to set up food camps and clothing drives. It was the most rewarding feeling to be able to help someone who was less fortunate and to contribute to eradicating child homelessness. I reflected back on the conversations I had with my grandfather, who said, "When you help someone who is less fortunate than you are, change will occur."

It was not until I served in Turkey that I became very serious about my purpose and passion in life. I knew that my ministry was in missions and serving the greater good because I felt an indescribable feeling every time I provided service in underserved communities. I learned this attribute from my grandfather. He was a great servant and impacted so many lives through his spirit of generosity and giving. I served in various ministries at the base chapel, including Usher Board, Young Adult Choir, and Men's Ministry. Upon my return to the States, I continued to serve in the Men's Ministry and Military Ministry at various churches, which provided me the opportunity to get involved in various initiatives, including mentoring young men, supporting the homeless, supporting veterans, and empowering youth. My last job in the military was in the Clinton administration in the Office of the Secretary of Defense, Public Affairs. Yes, Monica Lewinsky and I worked in the same office and knew each other! In this position, I began to place a great emphasis on mentoring young men of color. Many young men of color do not make it out of South Carolina, and the chances of making it to the Office of the Secretary of Defense in the Pentagon are slim to none. During that time, I was working on my master's degree, and I encouraged young men to earn the highest level of education possible to become empowered in all areas of their lives. I was capable of providing young men with this advice, as I had begun a path of healing to become self-empowered in many areas of my own life. I started mentoring young men in Washington, DC, public schools both personally and professionally. At this time, I knew my life had a greater purpose to impact change on a much larger scale than in the local communities I was serving.

When your life flashes before your eyes, you begin to reflect on how much greater you can be. I had this experience on 9/11 when the plane hit the Pentagon. I had been discharged from the military a few years prior and had begun my corporate career. I was working for Lockheed Martin in the Pentagon when the plane hit the building. I knew several of the people who were killed in the tragic event, and I continue to go to the Pentagon on 9/11 each year to commemorate with the families of the victims to celebrate the lives of their loved ones. As I look back over my life, I am thankful, and I declare the best gift that I have ever received was the gift of life. My birthday is September 12, and God spared me to see the day after 9/11 – another birthday. I am grateful for life, and I was later shown that my life is an example of how a person's past does not determine the future and how a person can transition from ordinary to extraordinary by creating a legacy and a body of work to change the world.

Throughout my 14-year corporate career, I continued to stay connected to service in some way. My last job in the corporate world was with Sodexo, where I was the senior director of organizational change for North America. In that role, I was also the national chairperson for HONOR, a military business resource group that consisted of over 500 military veterans and spouses. The focus of our strategy was to support and serve active, guard, and reserve military members and their spouses in the community. This was a rewarding way to serve the community because I had served 13 years in the Air Force and knew the challenges that military members had with transitioning from military to the corporate world and the lack of support they were provided after serving and protecting our country. I was able to partner with military organizations such as Paralyzed Veterans of America and Disabled American Veterans. During that time, I also served on the board of directors for Community for Creative Non-Violence in Washington, DC, which is the largest homeless shelter in the United States. While on the board, I worked with the homeless population, many of whom were veterans, on career development skills, life skills, and any support they needed to transition back into mainstream society.

During the process of earning my PhD and transitioning from the corporate world to higher education, my purpose and passion were confirmed and validated. I attended Walden University to earn my doctoral degree after speaking with a colonel I worked with in the Air Force who was working on completing his PhD there. He told me that he thought I should consider Walden because of my previous life's work in social change. The university was a perfect fit because the focus of Walden's mission is social change. While attending Walden, I connected with my purpose and passion more, and I began to use them both to impact positive change in the world on a global scale. While in the program, I began a cohort of doctoral students in the nation's capital and peer-mentored them in the area of research methods and provided them with resources and support to help them meet their educational goals and objectives. I later had job opportunities in higher education and a platform to mentor my own doctoral learners, and I increased graduation and retention rates at several universities. Thus, I have not only been able to encourage and empower young men of color to continue their education, but I have graduated men of color with PhDs – the highest level of education! This is impacting positive social change through purpose and passion by serving and mentoring! The peer-mentoring model has since been adopted by other universities, and results show that students have a greater chance of completing doctoral programs when they are in peer-mentoring and cohort models. In my 12 years in higher education, I have chaired dissertation committees and graduated over 100 doctoral students! I call them "McCollum Scholars!"

I have made a lifelong commitment to impacting positive social change in countries such as Costa Rica, South Africa, and Haiti. In Cahuita, Costa Rica, I led a delegation that assessed international development opportunities on an indigenous reservation and rebuilt homes to coincide with the Costa Rican culture of cooking over open fire. I also conducted workshops on leadership development and emotional intelligence to help locals have a greater understanding of mutual respect and self-dignity. In Komga, Eastern Cape, South Africa, I collaborated with an AIDS orphanage and local hospital to establish partnerships with U.S. organizations. I also mentored an educator in a local township on the teacher certification process and establishing a nonprofit organization.

After the devastation of the earthquake in Port au Prince, Haiti, I made a personal connection to the Haitian culture and its plight. The first time I went to Haiti was with a Christian organization on a missions trip. I have traveled to Haiti several times a year for the past 8 years. I have had the opportunity to do some great work in Haiti, which includes establishing a mentoring program for young men between the ages of 16 and 22 and coaching the young men on principles of servant leadership. I have also led delegations in Haiti to rebuild areas destroyed by natural disasters and explored opportunities to bring technology into the Haitian education system. I have had the opportunity to meet with the minister of education's cabinet on opportunities to pilot technology platforms in the school system. I am currently planning to build a primary school in Haiti to increase literacy and decrease poverty.

People often ask me why I do not invest in education in the United States instead of in Haiti. When you are clear on your purpose and passion, no one can deter you or discourage you to do otherwise. I am very clear that my eternal purpose and passion is to contribute to international development through mentoring and service. That clarity came through connecting with my faith early in my life, applying the foundational principles of service, and mentoring and becoming emotionally, culturally and spiritually intelligent. Emotional intelligence is paramount on the path to seeking clarity of purpose and passion. When you are self-aware about navigating your emotional landscape, you become more in tune with what motivates you intrinsically, you become more empathetic about using your life as a vehicle for change in the world, and you have a greater connection to managing social relationships. Cultural intelligence is also critical when you are on the path to seeking clarity of purpose and passion. When you immerse yourself in other cultures, you have a greater appreciation for the life you have and a greater understanding of the importance of embracing all of life's experiences, whether good or bad, and you can use the experiences as a means to contribute to the betterment of humankind!

The confirmation and validation of my purpose and passion were evident when I was selected as a Fulbright Scholar in 2015 through the Bureau of Educational and Cultural Affairs, State Department, Washington, DC, as a result of my international contributions. I was honored to join the ranks of over 250,000 Fulbright scholars who have made a significant contribution within various countries, as well as having the overall goal of advancing mutual understanding among cultures. My purpose and passion was also validated in 2016 when I worked with one of my former graduates, friend and colleague Dr. Dereje Tessema, to create and chair the International Conference on Interdisciplinary Research Studies, conducted at the George Washington University, Washington DC. The conference served as a platform to bring scholars, researchers, policy makers, organizational leaders, academics, and doctoral learners across multiple disciplines together to create and share knowledge regarding trends, best practices, and innovations related to solving complex world issues and challenges. Chairing this conference for two years provided an opportunity to impact lives and solve world problems through research.

Dr. Martin Luther King, Jr., said it best when he said, "Everyone cannot be famous, but everyone can be great. Greatness is shown through service." I hope to leave a legacy of greatness through my service contributions. I remember when my late grandfather, Walter D. McCollum, Sr., passed away and the pastor officiating the funeral placed his hands on my shoulder and said to me, "Receive a mantle of great works." My obligation is to continue my grandfather's legacy on a much larger scale. As an extension of his efforts, I am using my ordinary life to impact positive social change in extraordinary ways.

About the Author

Walter Ray McCollum, PhD
Fulbright Scholar

Dr. Walter McCollum is an executive, educator and international social change advocate. He has been employed by top companies, including Lucent Technologies, Booz Allen & Hamilton, Lockheed Martin, Science Application International Corporation (SAIC), Capgemini, and Sodexo.

Prior to working in the private sector, Dr. McCollum, a Desert Storm veteran, served 13 years in the U.S. Air Force, where he held various Air Force specialties in the areas of information management and communications. His military awards and medals include Air Force Commendation Medal w/1 Oak Leaf Cluster, Joint Meritorious Service Medal, Air Force Achievement Medal w/2 Oak Leaf Clusters, Southwest Asia Service Medal, Humanitarian Service Medal, National Defense Service Medal, Distinguished Graduate Noncommissioned Officer's Academy, Military Citizenship Award Noncommissioned Officer's Academy, and Office of the Secretary of Defense Junior Enlisted Member of the Year.

As a scholar-practitioner, Dr. McCollum has authored and published seven books: *Process Improvement in Quality Management Systems: Case Studies Analyzing Carnegie Mellon's Capability Maturity Model; Applied Change Management: Approaches to Organizational Change and Transformation; Strength of a Black Man: Destined for Self-Empowerment; Breakthrough Mentoring in the 21st Century: A Compilation of Life-Altering Experiences; How to Use Emotional, Cultural, and Spiritual Intelligence to Mentor Doctoral Learners; Purpose, Hope, and Determination: Transitioning from Ordinary to Extraordinary; and Black Men Changing the Narrative Through Education.* He is also published in several peer-reviewed journals.

Dr. McCollum has also been a professor at several universities, including New York University, Walden University, Northcentral University, Capella University, Upper Iowa University, Argosy University, University of Phoenix, University of the District of Columbia, Central Michigan University, and Colorado State University – Global. He holds a PhD in applied management and decision sciences with a specialization in leadership and organizational change from Walden University, an MA in management from Webster University, a BS in psychology from the State University of New York, Albany, and an AAS in Business Management from Dabney S. Lancaster Community College.

www.ingramcontent.com/pod-product-compliance
Lightning Source LLC
Chambersburg PA
CBHW042308150426

43198CB00001B/1